The Beatles
Unseen Archives

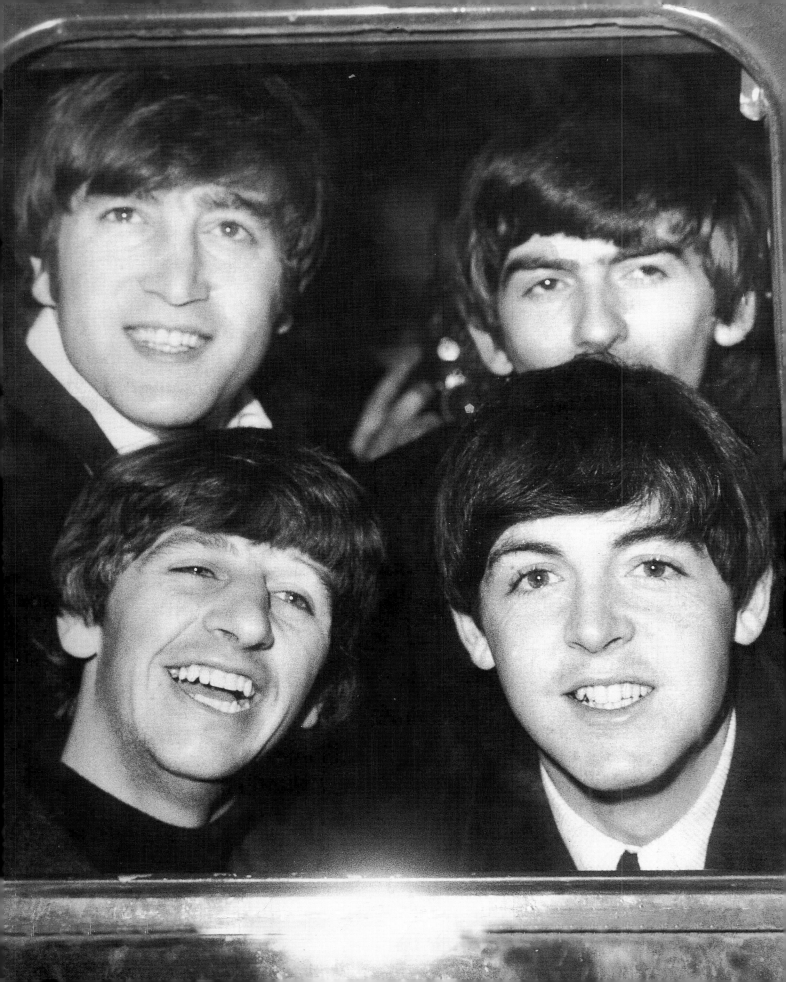

The Beatles
Unseen Archives

Photographs by the

Daily Mail

Compiled by

Tim Hill and Marie Clayton

p

This is a Parragon Book
This edition published in 2001

Parragon
Queen Street House
4 Queen Street
Bath, BA1 1HE, UK

Produced by Hazar Publishing Ltd

Designed by John Dunne
Origination by Croxons PrePress

A catalogue record for this book is available from the
British Library.
Hardback ISBN 0 75254 080 7
Paperback ISBN 0 75256 194 4

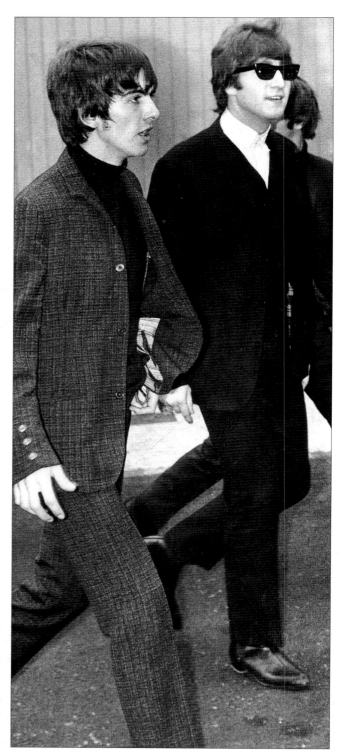

Contents

Introduction

Four lads who shook the world

Revisiting past glories and pleasures can often be an unrewarding experience. The glitter of any golden age tarnishes all too easily; the treasures of youth can appear dated and embarrassing just a few short years later. Those who were swept along with the tide of Osmondmania or Rollermania may have fond memories of the time, but it's doubtful whether the tartan cut-offs or 'Puppy Love' get much of an airing today.

The Beatles had more than their share of hype and hysteria; all the trappings and excesses of pop superstardom were there. They didn't have to play a note to send audiences into raptures and once the audience was in raptures, the notes were hardly worth playing. The deafening screams swamped the puny Vox amplifiers in those early days and the four of them sometimes gave in and stopped performing. The fans appeared not to realize - or to care.

But after Beatle jackets and haircuts were outgrown, after the flimflam and froth were stripped away, there remained the unique melding of four individual talents. They produced a canon of work with a timeless quality, music for all succeeding generations to discover and enthuse over. It is said that Brian Wilson, the creative genius behind the Beach Boys, abandoned the project he was working on after hearing *Sgt Pepper* for the first time. He didn't see the point of going on now that the definitive album had been made.

The Beatles not only dominated the musical landscape during their years together, but influenced it immeasurably after they went their separate ways. At the site of the original Cavern Club in Mathew Street there is a legend which puts it succinctly: 'Four lads who shook the world'. *The Beatles: Unseen Archives* recaptures that seismic phenomenon.

Acknowledgements

The Photographs from this book were taken by Associated Newspapers' photographers and are from the archives of the *Daily Mail*.

Many of these fabulous photographs, taken by some of the world's leading professionals, are from negatives never previously printed. The photographers' work has been carefully archived by the very dedicated staff in the Picture Library resulting in one of the last great remaining photographic treasures chronicling The Beatles.

The pleasure this book will give to the fans of the greatest rock band of the twentieth century is a tribute to the continued diligence and hard work of the team. Many thanks to David Sheppard and the present staff and all those who have held this important responsibility before them, including:

Brian Jackson	Oscar Courtney
Alan Pinnock	Andrew Young
John Bater	Rachel Swanston
Derek Johnson	David Lavington
David Stanley	Robert Sanders
Tom McElroy	Andrew Eva
Leslie Adler	Bill Beasley
Tony Fordham	Charles Whitbread
Steve Cooper	Philip Lambourne
Derek Drew	Carol Hooper
Steve Murray	Chris Nelthorpe
Raymond Archer	Denis Hoy
Terry Aylward	Bob Dignum
	Paul Howard

Thanks also to Christine Hoy, John Dunne, Cliff Salter, Lee Sherwood, Paul Rossiter, Richard Betts, Keith Lock, Ian Withers Alan Hatherly and Alison Gauntlett.

Particular thanks to Steve Torrington without whom this book would not have been possible.

Finally, thanks to the late Sir David English who was so inspirational and who would have enjoyed seeing the finished book.

The Beatles
Unseen Archives

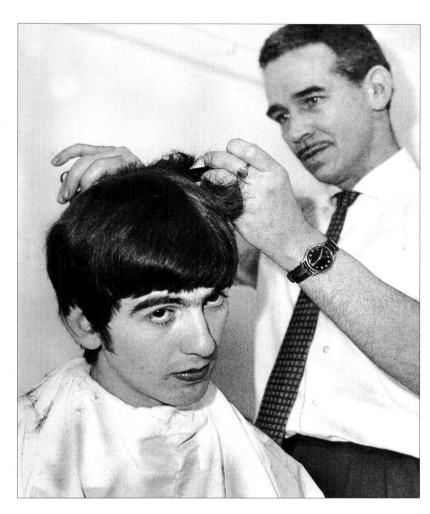

Chapter One

The Early Years

Ticket To Ride

Everyone knows that The Beatles came from Liverpool, but their distinctive sound and their talent for reaching an audience came not from the bars and clubs of their home town, but from their exhaustive stints far away in Hamburg. Until they went to Germany, the band was a constantly changing collection of part-time musicians, with a hard core of three members: John Lennon and Paul McCartney, both on rhythm guitar, and George Harrison on lead. They played anywhere they could – private parties, youth clubs, working men's clubs – not only changing the line-up regularly, but also experimenting with different names for the group.

Until 1960 the band had no permanent drummer or a bass guitarist, so when John's art-college friend Stu Sutcliffe won £60 in an art contest he was promptly persuaded to invest in a bass guitar even though he couldn't play. The band had earlier met local club-owner Allan Williams, who began to book them into gigs round Liverpool and even got them an audition which led to a short tour round Scotland, backing singer Johnny Gentle. In the middle of 1960, Williams was looking for another group to send to Hamburg and the only one available to go was... The Beatles. He offered them the booking, on condition they found themselves a competent drummer. One of their regular venues was the Casbah Club and Pete Best, son of the owner, had his own drum kit. He was quickly recruited into

The Beatles, and off they went to Germany.

In Hamburg the five Beatles – John, Paul, George, Stu and Pete – had to play ridiculously long hours every night in the same venue in front of demanding customers. They not only became a much more tightly-knit group, they also had to develop a dynamic stage presence and a louder, more raunchy playing style to satisfy the often drunken audience. Another major influence on their style was photographer Astrid Kirchherr, who took atmospheric pictures of them around the city and cut Stu's hair into the famous mop-top later adopted by John, Paul and George.

In addition, the band expanded their repertoire and came to know the songs so well that they were able to develop and perfect the sound that later took the world by storm. The line-up was also soon on its way to the final four: Stu left the group to live with Astrid, leaving Paul to take over bass guitar, and they became friendly with Ringo Starr, who was in Hamburg with Rory Storm and the Hurricanes. After The Beatles returned to Liverpool at the end of 1960, they were booked to appear at Litherland Town Hall. Their new sound and extrovert stage show exploded on to a stunned British audience, and things were never the same again.

It was not long before word of this dynamic new group spread round Liverpool and came to the ears of Brian Epstein, a local businessman and record-store owner. He came to see them at the Cavern Club one lunchtime and promptly decided he wanted to manage them – even though he had never managed a band before. He immediately took the boys in hand, making sure they turned up to bookings on time, tidying up their stage show and getting rid of their 'greasy rocker' image by banning their leather gear and putting them all into suits. He also started looking for a recording contract and finally got the group an audition at Decca – who turned them down. Brian was incensed, but he didn't give up and in May 1962 George Martin of Parlophone finally agreed to take them on.

One problem still remained – Martin was not keen on Pete Best's drumming style. This could perhaps have been resolved, but George, Paul and John took it as an opportunity to get rid of Pete, who they felt didn't fit in, and invite Ringo to join them instead. Pete had been with them for nearly two years but none of them was prepared to tell him to his face, so they left the task to Brian. It was all handled very badly.

Ringo joined The Beatles in mid-August, so he had just over two weeks of playing with them before they recorded their first single, 'Love Me Do'/'PS I Love You'. It was released in October and managed to reach No 17 in the charts – if rumors are to be believed, mainly because Brian Epstein bought up 10,000 copies.

Although The Beatles now had one record out and were due to appear on their first London TV program, they were still almost completely unknown outside Merseyside – but not for long. Throughout 1963 they worked a punishing schedule, which included four national British concert tours, two Scottish tours, one short Swedish tour and numerous one-night shows. They made two LPs, three EPs and four singles, a multitude of TV and radio recordings, and attended many photographic sessions and Press interviews. No reasonable request for their time was refused by Brian Epstein. Their second single was released early in the year and, after a rapid climb, hit the number-one spot towards the end of February. At the time The Beatles were on a tour supporting Helen Shapiro, but gradually they became the major attraction. For the following tour they were supposed to be supporting two American stars, Tommy Roe and Chris Montez, but soon took over as top of the bill.

In August, The Beatles gave their last-ever show at the Cavern; it could no longer contain the vast crowds of Beatle fans and anyway they had outgrown their local following. The BBC were not slow to pick up on the group's growing popularity: after many radio show appearances, the boys were offered their own radio series, *Pop Go The Beatles*, which ran over four weekly programs. The Beatles also appeared on BBC television so many times that cynics began to dub it the 'Beatles Broadcasting Corporation'. They already had their own

monthly magazine, *The Beatles Book*, and an official fan club, which had grown from a few thousand to 80,000 paid-up members by the end of 1963.

Even early in the year, Beatle-inspired mania had begun to break out locally around Britain, although it was only in October that the national newspapers finally began to pick up on the story. A live appearance by The Beatles on the network TV show, *Val Parnell's Sunday Night at the London Palladium*, which led to crowds of hysterical fans gathering outside the normally staid theater in the center of London, finally caught their attention. The next day the papers were full of stories about fans rioting and breaking through a police cordon when the boys tried to leave the theater. A couple of weeks later The Beatles returned to Heathrow airport from a short tour of Sweden and were stunned by the thousands of fans who had gathered in the rain to welcome them back, along with a full complement of reporters and photographers.

Since the national fame of The Beatles had arrived so suddenly, they soon found themselves having to fulfil bookings made months previously for fees that were ludicrously low in comparison to what they could now command. Brian Epstein did occasionally try to buy them out of some of these dates if he thought that the proposed venue would no longer be safe, but otherwise he never went back on a signed contract. A much more serious problem was the increasingly manic behavior of the fans, which had now become dangerous both to themselves and the group. Girls cried, screamed, tried to throw themselves at their favorite Beatle or grab pieces of clothing or snippets of hair, or simply fainted. Even in the small town of Carlisle, 600 fans queued for up to 36 hours in freezing weather for the box office to open. When it did, the surge forward resulted in nine people being taken to hospital. At larger venues the casualties sometimes ran into hundreds. It was a major logistical exercise to get the band to and from the venue in safety, and once inside they had to stay cooped up in their dressing-rooms, prisoners of their own fame. When thay actually made it onto the stage, they had to dodge around to avoid being hit by the gifts and packets of jelly babies thrown by fans.

For The Beatles themselves the growing Beatlemania was at first flattering, but quickly went beyond a joke and began to be a cause of some resentment. Concert tours were already a mind-numbing routine of arriving in a town, being smuggled into the venue, performing a show, being hustled out into a van for a high-speed getaway to a nearby hotel, and then holing up overnight until it was time to go through it all again the next day. They had to wear elaborate disguises to go out in public, their homes and those of their families were under constant siege from fans, articles were stolen from their dressing-rooms and the piercing screams throughout concerts meant that no one – not even The Beatles themselves – could hear the music.

But they had already changed the British music scene for ever. Before this, popular musical trends had invariably started in America and major stars were American, while London had a stranglehold on the British scene. Now Liverpool suddenly became fashionable and Merseyside took over the pop charts. Gerry and the Pacemakers, Cilla Black, the Searchers, Billy J. Kramer and the Dakotas all owed their success to The Beatles - and most of them were also managed by Brian Epstein.

Previous page: The sweet smile of success. At the end of 1962, Brian Epstein had been buying up copies of 'Love Me Do' by the bucketload to ensure chart success; within a few short months, advance copies of Beatles records were selling in their hundreds of thousands.

Below: The Beatles are very thinly disguised as policemen in order to get past the huge crowds gathering for a concert outside the Birmingham Hippodrome.

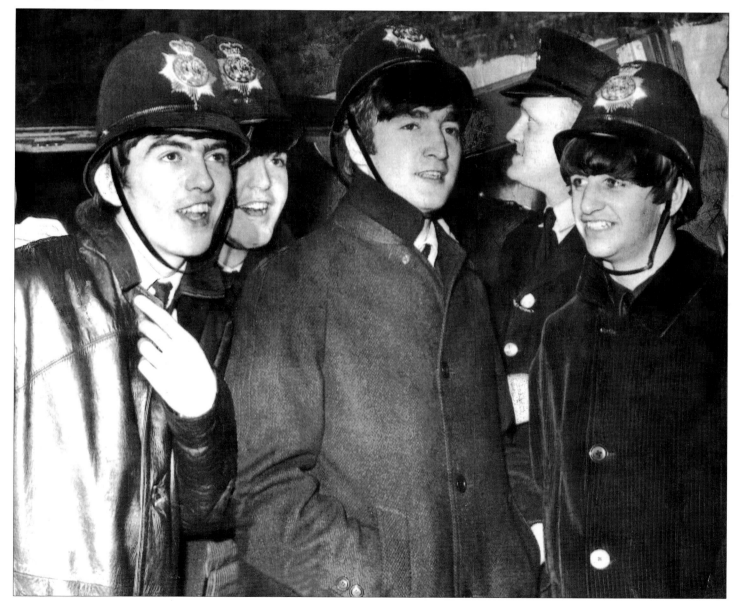

The Early Years: Chronology

1934

19 September	Brian Epstein is born in Liverpool

1939

10 September	Cynthia Powell is born in Blackpool

1940

23 June	Stuart Sutcliffe is born in Edinburgh, Scotland
7 July	Ringo Starr is born at the Royal Liverpool Children's Hospital
9 October	John Lennon is born at the Oxford Street Maternity Hospital, in Liverpool

1941

24 January	Randolph Peter Best is born in Madras, India

1942

18 June	Paul McCartney is born at Walton Hospital, Liverpool

1943

25 February	George Harrison is born at home at 12 Arnold Grove, Wavertree, Liverpool

1957

March	John forms The Black Jacks skiffle group with Pete Shotton, which is later renamed The Quarry Men
9 June	The Quarry Men audition for Carroll Levis' *TV Star Search* at Liverpool's Empire Theatre, but fail to qualify
6 July	Paul meets John for the first time, when he sees The Quarry Men play at St Peter's Church garden fete in Liverpool
20 July	Paul is invited to join The Quarry Men
7 August	The Quarry Men perform at the Cavern Club in Liverpool for the first time
18 October	Paul's debut performance with The Quarry Men, at the New Clubmore Hall, Liverpool. He played lead guitar, but made a mess of his solo and was demoted to rhythm

1958

6 February	George meets The Quarry Men and is later invited to join them because of his growing skill as a guitarist, although he is younger than the others
15 July	Julia, John's mother, is killed by a speeding car when crossing the road after leaving his Aunt Mimi's house

1959

25 March	Ringo joins Rory Storm and the Hurricanes, at that time Merseyside's top band
29 August	The Quarry Men play at the opening night of the Casbah Club, owned by Pete Best's mother. The group consists of John, Paul, George and Ken Brown. They still have no drummer
10 October	Ken Brown quits The Quarry Men
15 November	As Johnny and the Moondogs, John, Paul and George make the final audition for Carroll Levis' *TV Star Search* at Liverpool's Empire Theatre

1960

January	Stuart Sutcliffe, a friend of John at the Art College, joins The Quarry Men as bass player
May	The Quarry Men become The Beatals
10 May	The Beatals become The Silver Beetles and audition as a backing group for Billy Fury, but instead are booked to tour Scotland as backing for singer Johnny Gentle
20-28 May	The Silver Beetles tour Scotland. The group have also changed their own names: 'Long John' Lennon, Paul Ramon (McCartney), Carl (George) Harrison and Stu de Stael (Stuart Sutcliffe). Tommy Moore (his real name) plays the drums
June	The Silver Beetles become The Beatles before reverting to The Silver Beetles
July	The Silver Beetles become The Silver Beatles
12 August	Pete Best joins The Silver Beatles as drummer
16 August	The group finally becomes The Beatles and sets off for Hamburg
17 Aug-3 Oct	The Beatles play at the Indra Club on Hamburg's Grosse Freiheit
4 Oct-30 Nov	The Beatles play at the Kaiserkeller Club
15 October	John, Paul, George and Ringo record together for the first time, with bassist Walter Eymond of Rory Storm and the Hurricanes, at Akustic Studio, Hamburg
10 November	John leaves Hamburg
21 November	George is deported from West Germany for being under-age for nightclub work after midnight
29 November	Paul and Pete are thrown into jail for apparently setting fire to their living quarters at the Bambi cinema
30 November	Paul and Pete are released from jail but deported. Stu stays in Germany with his girlfriend, Astrid Kirchherr
27 December	The Beatles perform at the Litherland Town Hall in Liverpool, inciting the first scenes of Beatlemania

1961

9 February	The Beatles perform for the first time at the Cavern Club, in a lunchtime session

21 March	The Beatles perform for the first time in an evening session at the Cavern	3 December	The Beatles attend their first business meeting with Brian Epstein, at his record store
27 Mar–2 Jul	The Beatles make their second trip to Hamburg, to play at the Top Ten Club on the Reeperbahn	6 December	Brian Epstein offers to manage the group and John accepts on their behalf
22–23 June	The Beatles play in a professional recording studio for the first time, backing singer Tony Sheridan and performing a couple of numbers without him for producer Bert Kaempfert	9 December	The Beatles play their first concert down south at the Palais Ballroom, Aldershot, but it is not advertised so only 18 people turn up
9 November	Brian Epstein visits the Cavern Club at lunchtime to see The Beatles performing	13 December	A&R man Mike Smith of Decca Records comes to see The Beatles play at the Cavern Club

Below: George sends another autograph-hunter away happy. The first Harrison song to feature on a Beatles record is 'Don't Bother Me' on the new LP, *With The Beatles*. He would later describe it as a 'crappy' song, instantly forgettable. It would be two years before he would contribute another song to The Beatles' canon, on the *Help!* album.

1962

1 January	The Beatles audition for Mike Smith and Dick Rowe at Decca, recording 15 songs
4 January	The Beatles top a popularity poll in local music paper, *Mersey Beat*
24 January	The Beatles sign a management contract with Brian Epstein, although Epstein himself does not sign
February	Decca Records turn down The Beatles
13 February	Brian Epstein meets George Martin, EMI Records' head of A&R, and plays him the recording of The Beatles' failed Decca audition
7 March	The Beatles make their radio debut, recording at Manchester's Playhouse Theatre for the BBC's *Teenager's Turn (Here We Go)*, which is transmitted the following day
10 April	Stuart Sutcliffe dies of a brain hemorrhage aged 21
13 Apr–31 May	The Beatles make their third trip to Hamburg, to perform at the new Star-Club on Grosse Freiheit
9 May	Brian Epstein meets George Martin again, and The Beatles are offered a recording contract, depending on an audition/recording session scheduled for 6 June
6 June	The Beatles perform the audition/recording session at EMI studios in Abbey Road and are formally offered a record deal
15 August	Ringo is invited to join The Beatles and accepts
16 August	Pete Best is fired as The Beatles' drummer
18 August	Ringo makes his debut as a Beatle, at Hulme Hall in Port Sunlight, Birkenhead
22 August	The Beatles are filmed at the Cavern by Granada Television, but the footage is shelved until they become famous the following year
23 August	John marries Cynthia Powell at Liverpool's Mount Pleasant Register Office
4 September	The Beatles return to Abbey Road for their first formal recording session with Ringo
1 October	Brian Epstein finally signs the management contract with The Beatles
5 October	Their first single, 'Love Me Do'/'PS I Love You', is released in the UK and reaches No 17 in the charts
17 October	The Beatles make their TV debut with a live appearance on Granada Television's *People And Places*, which was broadcast to the north and north-west
1-14 Nov	The Beatles' fourth season in Hamburg, a two-week booking to play at the Star-Club
18-31 Dec	The Beatles' fifth and final stint in Hamburg, again playing at the Star-Club

1963

2-6 January	The Beatles travel around Scotland for their first concert tour
11 January	Their second single, 'Please Please Me'/'Ask Me Why', is released in the UK (25 February in the US)
19 January	The Beatles make their national TV debut on *Thank Your Lucky Stars*, playing 'Please Please Me'
2 February	The Beatles begin their first proper package tour of Britain, supporting Helen Shapiro
2 February	The first London newspaper coverage of The Beatles appears in the *Evening Standard*, a general feature by Maureen Cleave
11 February	The Beatles record ten new tracks for their first album, *Please Please Me*, in just under ten hours
19 February	The 'Please Please Me' single tops both the *New Musical Express* and *Disc* magazine charts, although it only reaches No 2 on the BBC chart
9 March	The Beatles embark on their second British concert tour, supporting Chris Montez and Tommy Roe
22 March	Their first LP, *Please Please Me*, is released in the UK and tops the British charts
5 April	The Beatles receive their first silver disk, for selling 250,000 copies of their single, 'Please Please Me'
8 April	John and Cynthia have a son, John Charles Julian
11 April	The Beatles' third single, 'From Me To You'/'Thank You Girl', is released in the UK (27 May in the US). It is the first of eleven consecutive singles to top the British charts through to 1966
18 April	Paul meets young actress Jane Asher after a BBC radio concert broadcast live from the Royal Albert Hall
18 May	The Beatles start their third British tour
4 June	A BBC radio series, *Pop Go The Beatles*, is launched
21 June	'Beatle in brawl' headline appears in the *Daily Mirror*, reporting that John got drunk and beat up Cavern DJ Bob Wooler at Paul's 21st birthday party in Liverpool on 18 April
12 July	The EP *Twist And Shout* is released in the UK
16 July	The Beatles record 17 songs for three separate episodes of their show, *Pop Go The Beatles*
22 July	The LP *Introducing The Beatles* is first released in the US only. It is re-released in the US on 27 January 1964
1 August	Publication of the first issue of *The Beatles Book*, a monthly magazine about the group
3 August	The Beatles play for the last time at the Cavern Club
13 August	The EP *Twist And Shout* sells 250,000 copies and becomes the first of its genre to qualify for silver status
23 August	The single 'She Loves You'/'I'll get You' is released in the UK (16 September in the US)
3 September	The Beatles record a further 18 songs for another three separate episodes of *Pop Go The Beatles*
6 September	The EP *The Beatles' Hits* is released in the UK
10 September	The Beatles receive the award for Top Vocal Group of the Year at the Variety Club Awards lunch at the Savoy hotel
15 September	The Beatles share the bill with the Rolling Stones at the annual *Great Pop Prom* at the Royal Albert Hall, London
5 October	A three-day tour of Scotland begins at the Concert Hall, Glasgow
13 October	A live appearance by The Beatles on the network TV show, *Val Parnell's Sunday Night at the London Palladium*, causes a sensation across Britain
23 October	The Beatles fly to Sweden for their first proper foreign concert tour
31 October	Thousands of fans gather at London Airport to greet The Beatles on their return from Sweden

1 November	First night of The Beatles' Autumn Tour of Britain, in Cheltenham, Gloucestershire
1 November	The EP *The Beatles (No 1)* is released in the UK
2 November	The *Daily Mirror* coins the term 'Beatlemania', when reviewing the Cheltenham show
4 November	The Beatles appear at the *Royal Variety Performance*, where John asks the audience to rattle their jewellery
6 November	The footage filmed by Granada Television at the Cavern Club in 1962 is finally shown on *Scene At 6.30*
9 November	George signs a five-year music publishing contract with Northern Songs
9 November	After their show in East Ham, The Beatles go to a party in London given by millionaire John Bloom
16 November	Clark's Grammar School in Guildford, Surrey becomes the first school to send boys home for sporting a Beatles haircut
22 November	The LP *With The Beatles* is released in the UK
29 November	The single 'I Want To Hold Your Hand'/'This Boy' is released in the UK. In the US the B side is 'I Saw Her Standing There' and the single is released on 26 December
24 December	*The Beatles' Christmas Show* begins at the Astoria Cinema, Finsbury Park, London. It runs for 16 nights

Below: George dances the night away at a party given by millionaire John Bloom.

'I haven't seen anything like this...'

Paul and John's prodigious songwriting talent comes to the fore in 1963. They begin the year by stubbornly refusing George Martin's suggestion to record 'How Do You Do It?' as a follow-up to 'Love Me Do', insisting on writing their own material. (Gerry and the Pacemakers were subsequently offered the song and took it to No 1 in the charts.)

Below: After their triumphant appearance on *Sunday Night at the London Palladium*, the boys try to wrong-foot fans by leaving via the front exit, rather than the stage door. Ringo, John, Paul and road manager Neil Aspinall show concern as they emerge to find no waiting vehicle.

Opposite above: The getaway car has been parked some way up Argyll Street, where police hoped it would look less conspicuous. By the time Paul and Ringo reach it, the fans are in hot pursuit. 'I haven't seen anything like this since Johnny Ray appeared in 1955,' said George Cooper, the theatre's stage doorman.

Opposite below: The Beatles in an off-duty moment at a TV studio in Birmingham. The hectic touring commitments continue, but Epstein recognizes the impact of television exposure. Record sales quadruple on the day following the *Palladium* appearance, and Epstein is already targeting the top-rated *Ed Sullivan Show* as a bridgehead for The Beatles' assault on America.

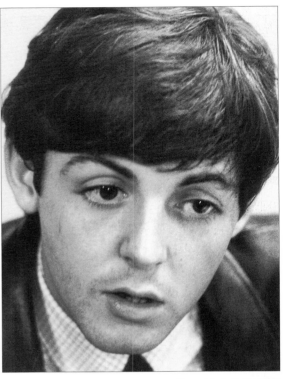

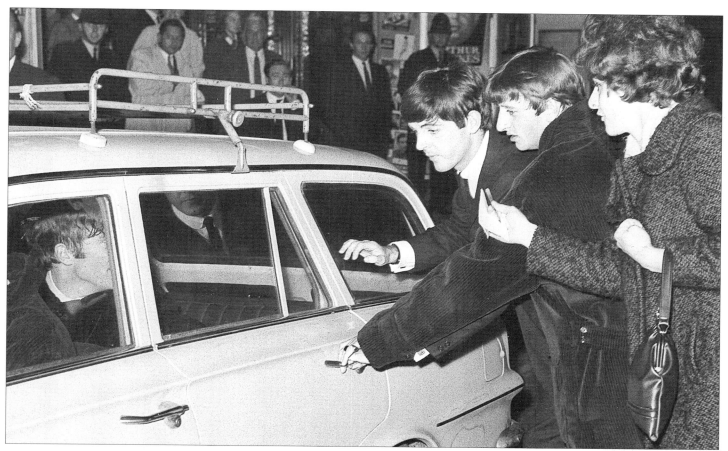

'Rattle your jewellery'

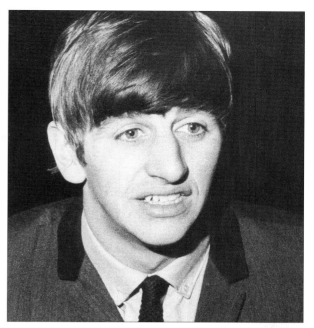

Opposite and right: Thousands of fans gather at London Airport as the Beatles return from a five-day trip to Sweden. They create a bigger security headache than Prime Minister Sir Alec Douglas-Home, who happens to be passing through the airport at the same time. By pure chance, one witness to the chaotic scenes is the very person Epstein wants to do business with - Ed Sullivan himself.

Below: Rehearsing on 4 November for the *Royal Variety Performance* at the Prince of Wales Theatre. The nineteen-act bill includes Max Bygraves, Harry Secombe, Tommy Steele, Marlene Dietrich and Pinky and Perky. The Beatles are seventh on stage but, predictably, steal the show with a set comprising 'From Me To You', 'She Loves You', 'Till There Was You' and 'Twist and Shout'. However, the evening is probably best remembered for the celebrated 'ad lib' with which John introduces the final number: 'Will those in the cheaper seats clap your hands; the rest of you can just rattle your jewellery.'

Mop-tops...

Below: Close-up mop-top. Beatles wigs are just one example of the vast merchandising industry which accompanies Beatlemania. Epstein fails to realize the full potential of this market. He enters into an agreement in which 90% of merchandising profits go to a company set up to handle all such matters.One of the earliest deals was with a clothing company which paid $100,000 for the right to produce Beatle T-shirts. Epstein thought this sum ludicrous, until he discovered that the company recouped this outlay in just three days. It would be 1967 before this disastrous arrangement was ended, by which time it was estimated that The Beatles had lost $100 million.

Right and opposite: Ringo dances with music publisher's wife Mrs Lou Levy at a Mayfair party given by millionaire John Bloom. 68-year-old porter Arthur Dyer proves to be slightly out of touch with popular culture by refusing to let The Beatles in at first, believing them to be gatecrashers instead of VIP guests.

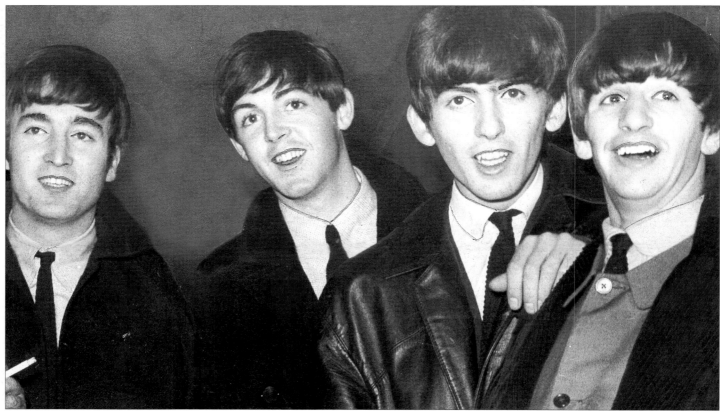

A quiet night out

Paul's hopes for a quiet evening out with Jane Asher are dashed as he becomes the centre of attention at a West End theatre.

Opposite: There is no better endorsement for a garment than to have a Beatle wear it. Here, as the boys arrive for a concert in Huddersfield, Ringo sports a corduroy coat. The ailing corduroy industry is said to have The Beatles to thank for a huge growth in sales during this period.

Flying high
in the charts

Swapping a drumstick for a joystick. Ringo tries his hand at the controls of the Viking aircraft taking some of the biggest names in pop from Liverpool to London. Brian Epstein had chartered the plane at a cost of £400 to give Ringo and other members of his Mersey Sound stable a break from *The Beatles' Christmas Show*, at the Astoria, Finsbury Park.

The Beatles had cause to be pleased with themselves in December '63. Advance sales of their new single, 'I Want To Hold Your Hand', hit the one million mark, while orders for the new LP *With The Beatles* stand at 250,000 - a record for an album.

Chapter Two

1964

A Hard Day's Night

If 1963 was the year that Beatlemania hit Britain, 1964 was the year when The Beatles conquered the rest of the world. Their first stop was Paris, but the shows here were not a success. The Beatles themselves were not satisfied with how things were organized, nor with their playing at the first concert, and one of the amplifiers cut out so many times that sabotage was suspected. The audience at the second concert was mainly Parisiennes in evening dress, rather than young rock fans, so the band received a cool reception. This was the concert the French Press attended, so reviews were similarly cool. These problems did not affect them long, however, as news suddenly came by telegram that 'I Want To Hold Your Hand' had shot from No 43 to No 1 in the music charts in America.

Soon all the group's records were climbing up the American charts - just days before they were due to visit New York to appear on *The Ed Sullivan Show* and to give concerts at the Washington Coliseum and Carnegie Hall. Their reception at John F. Kennedy Airport was wildly enthusiastic, as America succumbed to The Beatles in a typically whole-hearted fashion. The viewing figures for *The Ed Sullivan Show* smashed the existing world record for the largest-ever audience for an entertainment show, and during The Beatles' ten-minute spot there were no hub caps reported stolen in New York - which was also a first!

As well as visiting New York and Washington The Beatles also spent a few days in Miami, where they not only appeared live on *The Ed Sullivan Show* again and taped a third performance to be shown later, but also managed a few days of rest and relaxation. Wherever the boys went the now-familiar scenes of pandemonium unfolded yet again as American fans went crazy.

After their brief visit to America, the group returned home to begin their first film, *A Hard Day's Night*, at Twickenham. The storyline was based on incidents from their own lives, with all four Beatles playing their parts with great confidence. Meanwhile, Beatlemania was taking hold across the rest of the world. By the beginning of April, Beatles singles occupied the top five positions in the American *Billboard* chart and the top six positions in the singles charts in Sydney.

After four weeks off in May, the longest rest The Beatles had managed for some considerable time, they were ready to begin their first world tour, starting in Denmark. The day before their departure Ringo collapsed during a photo-shoot and was rushed to hospital suffering from tonsillitis and pharyngitis. Although George felt that they couldn't go without Ringo and wanted to cancel the tour, Brian Epstein and George Martin persuaded him that this was impossible. Instead, Jimmy Nicol, a very experienced but relatively unknown session drummer, became the temporary replacement for Ringo. Just hours after Ringo's collapse, Nicol went to EMI's

Abbey Road studios to rehearse six numbers with the world's greatest supergroup and the following day he was on his way to Denmark.

Beatlemania now followed the band wherever they appeared, not just at the concert venues in Denmark, The Netherlands, Hong Kong, Australia and New Zealand but also wherever the plane touched down for refuelling. Day or night, in even the remotest of places, crowds of screaming fans appeared out of nowhere to try and catch a glimpse of their idols. Ringo rejoined The Beatles in Australia, just in time for their first concert in Melbourne. Their reception across the country was even more manic than it had been in America: in Melbourne, an estimated 250,000 people gathered outside their hotel and in Adelaide the crowd was over 300,000 – many more than had ever turned out to see them in either Britain or even in America.

After a few bookings in Britain and another short tour to Sweden, The Beatles then set off on their first full American tour. It consisted of 32 shows in 24 cities within 34 days - which would perhaps have been reasonable in Britain, but was far too much in a land the size of America. John, Paul, George and Ringo spent almost the entire time travelling and, except for journeying to and from concert venues and airports, they were unable to leave their hotels. They saw very little of any of the places they visited, only the crowds of rampaging fans everywhere they went.

Kansas City was not originally included in the tour, but Charles O. Finlay, the millionaire president of the Kansas City Athletics baseball team, was determined to get The Beatles for his city and offered the unprecedented sum of $150,000 for them to appear for one night at Kansas City Stadium. After their visit, the 16 sheets and eight pillowcases from their hotel beds were sold to two Chicago businessmen for $750. The linen was left unlaundered, cut into three-inch squares, mounted on a card with a legal affidavit and sold at $10 a time. The towels used by The Beatles to mop their faces after the concert were also cut up and sold.

When The Beatles returned to Britain from America, to the usual hysterical scenes at London Airport, the Prime Minister, Sir Alec Douglas-Home, called them 'our best exports' and 'a useful contribution to the balance of payments'.

Below: Seeing double - The Beatles and their wax-work equivalents at Madame Tussaud's.
Previous page: Paul, George, Ringo and John enjoy some winter sunshine in Miami at the end of their first trip to the USA.

1964: Chronology

3 January	A clip of The Beatles is shown on *The Jack Paar Show* in the US
15 January	The Beatles perform in Versailles, France, before starting a two-week season at the Olympia Theatre in Paris
20 January	The LP *Meet The Beatles* is released in the US
25 January	In America's *Cashbox* magazine, 'I Want To Hold Your Hand' jumps 43 places to top the singles chart
30 January	The single 'Please Please Me' is re-released in the US only, with 'From Me To You' as the B side
7 February	The EP *All My Loving* is released in the UK
7 February	The Beatles arrive at Kennedy Airport in New York
9 February	The Beatles make a landmark television appearance on *The Ed Sullivan Show*, watched by 73 million viewers
11 February	The Beatles' US debut concert, at the Washington Coliseum
12 February	Two more concerts, at Carnegie Hall back in New York
12 February	A hastily-made documentary about The Beatles' US visit is shown on UK television
13 February	The Beatles fly from New York to Miami, to do their second *Ed Sullivan Show* and have a few days off to relax
16 February	The second *Ed Sullivan Show* featuring The Beatles is watched by 70 million viewers
22 February	The Beatles return to England
2 March	A single, 'Twist And Shout'/'There's A Place', is released in the US only
2 March	The Beatles begin shooting their first film, *A Hard Day's Night*
10 March	Ringo does the pub sequences for the film in Twickenham
16 March	The single 'Can't Buy Me Love'/'You Can't Do That' is released in the US (20 March in the UK)
19 March	The Beatles collect their Variety Club of Great Britain 1963 Showbusiness Personalities of the Year award
23 March	The Duke of Edinburgh presents The Beatles with Carl-Alan awards
23 March	John's first book, *In His Own Write*, is published and the first print run quickly sells out
23 March	A single, 'Do You Want to Know a Secret'/'Thank You Girl', is released in the US
3 April	The Beatles hold the top six positions in a singles chart in Sydney, Australia
4 April	Beatles singles are also in the top five positions in America's *Billboard* chart
10 April	An LP, *The Beatles' Second Album*, is released in the US
23 April	John attends a Foyle's literary luncheon in his honour
27 April	A single, 'Love Me Do'/'PS I Love You', is released in the US
29 April	The Beatles arrive in Scotland for two concerts
6 May	ITV screen their own TV special, *Around The Beatles*
21 May	A single, 'Sie Liebt Dich'/'I'll Get You', is released in the US
May	Madame Tussaud's unveil their models of The Beatles
3 June	Ringo collapses with tonsillitis and pharyngitis just prior to The Beatles' first world tour. He is temporarily replaced by session drummer Jimmy Nicol
4 June	The world tour begins with a concert in Copenhagen, Denmark
11 June	The Beatles arrive in Sydney, Australia
15 June	Ringo rejoins The Beatles in Australia and performs with them from Melbourne onwards
19 June	The EP *Long Tall Sally* is released in the UK
26 June	The LP *A Hard Day's Night* is released in the US (10 July in the UK)
6 July	*A Hard Day's Night* has its royal world charity première at the London Pavilion cinema
10 July	The single, 'A Hard Day's Night'/'Things We Said Today', is released in the UK. In the US the B side is 'I Should Have Known Better' and the single is released on 13 July
12 July	A concert at the Hippodrome, Brighton, is the first of five summer concerts at British seaside resorts
20 July	Two singles, 'I'll Cry Instead'/'I'm Happy Just to Dance With You' and 'And I Love Her'/'If I Fell' are released in the US
20 July	An LP, *Something New*, is released in the US
23 July	The Beatles appear in a charity show, *The Night of A Hundred Stars*, at the London Palladium
18 August	The Beatles leave London Airport for their first US concert tour
24 August	A single, 'Matchbox'/'Slow Down', is released in the US
17 September	The Beatles are paid $150,000 to play Kansas City Municipal Stadium on their day off, earning around £1,785 per minute
9 October	Another UK tour begins at the Gaumont Cinema, Bradford. The Beatles are joined by Motown star, Mary Wells
6 November	The EP *Extracts From The Film A Hard Day's Night* is released in the UK
6 November	The EP *Extracts From The Album A Hard Day's Night* is released in the UK
8 November	The first concert in Liverpool for nearly a year is held at the Liverpool Empire
23 November	An LP, *The Beatles' Story*, is released in the US
23 November	The single, 'I Feel Fine'/'She's A Woman', is released in the US (27 November in the UK)
1 December	Ringo holds a Press conference about his tonsils
4 December	The LP *Beatles For Sale* is released in the UK
15 December	A different LP, *Beatles '65*, is released in the US
24 December	*Another Beatles Christmas Show* begins at the Odeon, Hammersmith and runs until 16 January 1965

She loves you...

Below: George takes advantage of a brief respite in the relentless schedule to return home to Liverpool.

Harold and Louise Harrison help him pack for the America trip. Some of George's gear goes into his 'BEA-TLES' travel bag, the airline company's latest merchandising gimmick. In return for displaying the bags prominently, the boys were given free flights between London and Paris.

Below right: He gets a kiss from proud mum and number one fan Louise, who encouraged his early efforts with the guitar and attended a lot of the early gigs.

Opposite: John and George on their way to France, where lukewarm audiences get the year off to an inauspicious start.

Right: Singer Sylvie Vartan tries out one of Ringo's cameras during the Beatles' 18-day residency at the Olympia Theatre, Paris. Both Vartan and American singer Trini Lopez go down better than The Beatles with the French audiences, but the boys are buoyed by the news that they have become the first British group to top the US charts with 'I Want to Hold Your Hand'.

The Beatles Are Coming!

The Lennons at London Airport, preparing to fly out to New York. The fact that one of the Beatles was married with a child had only recently been uncovered by prying Fleet Street reporters.

Opposite above: 'The Beatles Are Coming!' That was the message on hoardings and on the airwaves right across the USA.

Opposite below: Apart from the two *Ed Sullivan Show* appearances, The Beatles give just three performances during their 15-day America trip: one concert at Washington Coliseum, and two shows at Carnegie Hall.

Washington

The Washington venue had the boys on a revolving stage. This had unfortunate consequences, for it not only afforded the whole audience a better view, but it also made the group a target to a lot more people. It had been reported that George had a particular weakness for jelly babies; this fondness proved painful in Washington, for the stage was peppered from all angles with these mini-missiles.

Drowned out

The Beatles were doing their best to belt out their material, but
their Vox amplifiers were nowhere near up to the task in a venue
full of screaming teenagers.

Look this way boys...

More photo calls on their flying visit.

The two Carnegie Hall concerts are hugely successful and massively over-subscribed, and as a result there was a last-minute attempt to organize a show at Madison Square Garden - at double the Carnegie Hall fee - but this proved impossible.

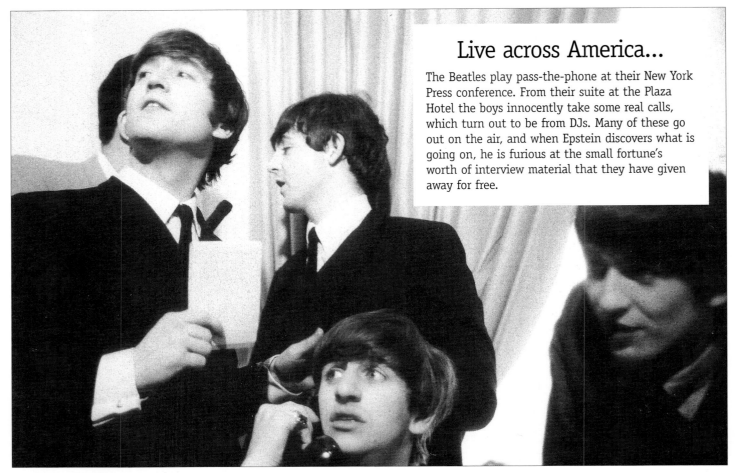

Live across America...

The Beatles play pass-the-phone at their New York Press conference. From their suite at the Plaza Hotel the boys innocently take some real calls, which turn out to be from DJs. Many of these go out on the air, and when Epstein discovers what is going on, he is furious at the small fortune's worth of interview material that they have given away for free.

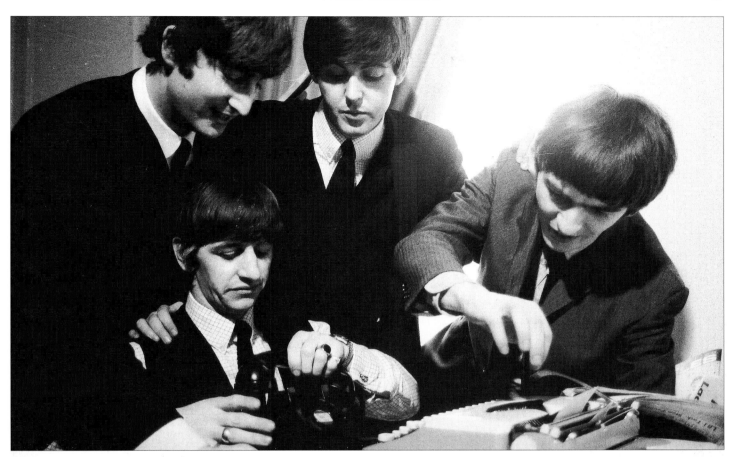

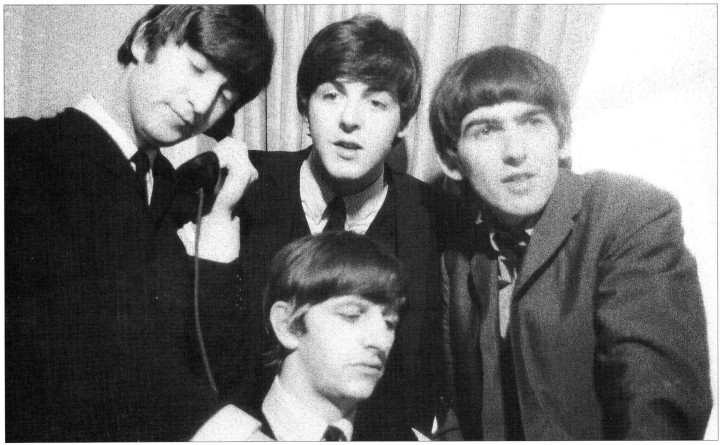

A room with a view

The Beatles in their suite at the Plaza Hotel keep an eye on the fans outside.

Opposite: Bad weather means that the flight from New York to Washington is cancelled, so The Beatles are forced to go by train.

Seeing the sights

Only a few photographers and interested onlookers are on hand as The Beatles see the sights of the capital.

'Not quite hopeless'

Reviews of *The Ed Sullivan Show* are mixed, including this from the New York Journal-American: 'Sartorially they're silly, tonsorially they're wildly sloppy, musically they're not quite hopeless'. The estimated 73 million audience begs to differ.

Epstein had targeted the top-rated show to get exposure for the group, after 'Love Me Do', 'Please Please Me' and 'She Loves You' had all failed to make an impression. The *Sullivan Show* wanted the Beatles as a novelty support act; Epstein wanted a top-of-the-bill slot. The deal ultimately thrashed out - headlining two shows on consecutive weeks for a total fee of just $7000. Epstein used the show as a huge loss-leader in order to break into the US market.

Opposite: All aboard in Miami.

Miami

A far cry from ferrying across the Mersey. The boys go cruising off the Miami coast aboard the luxury yacht *Southern Trail*. Their second appearance on *The Ed Sullivan Show*, on 16 February, is another triumph, with the audience again hitting the 70 million mark.

Miami beach boys

The fact that the schedule during the visit is, by Beatles' standards, not very onerous leaves the boys plenty of time to hit Miami beach before their second appearance on the *Sullivan Show*.

The dignified distance that most of the onlookers keep belies the frenzy that sweeps across America during this first visit. Anything Beatle-related is suddenly in demand and over half a ton of Beatle wigs and 24,000 rolls of Beatle wallpaper are quickly flown to America.

Fast sellers...

In the US, 'I Want To Hold Your Hand' had become the fastest-selling single to date when it sold 250,000 copies within the first three days of its release. In March, 'Can't Buy Me Love' was released with advance orders of over two million in the US alone.

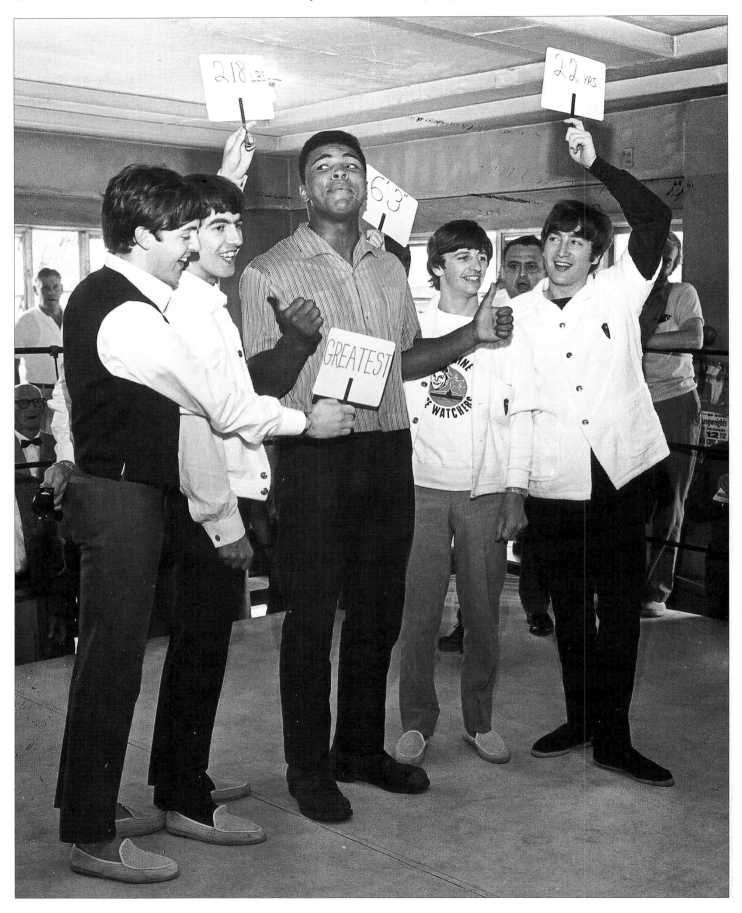

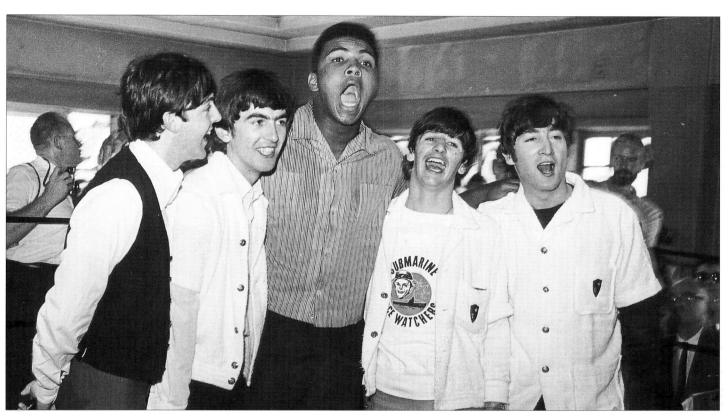

The Greatest

The Beatles come up against Cassius Clay, who is in Miami for his 25 February world title showdown with Sonny Liston. Clay declares that he's still the greatest, but The Beatles are the prettiest. Both parties come to world prominence in 1964 and go on to dominate their respective fields for the rest of the decade.

The Beatles returned to England on 22 February. A 36-minute documentary programme on their US visit was shown on British television while they were away.

Above: Waiting for 'The Greatest', Cassius Clay.

Below and opposite: Making a publicity appearance in the US under the watchful eye of Brian Epstein.

21 today!

George receives 52 sacks of mail containing 15,000 cards on his 21st birthday. Presents inevitably include endless packets of jelly babies, but one fan sends a full-sized door for George to put his 21st birthday key in.

Opposite above: Helping George to deal with the mountain of mail are Beatles' Fan Club secretaries Anne Collingham (*left*) and Bettina Rose.

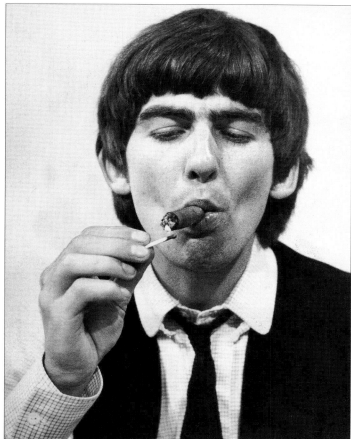

George's jam butties...

Opposite below: With filming for *A Hard Day's Night* just under way, the boys are invited to dine at Brasenose College, Oxford. John recollects his Chaucer studies at school; George trades his smoked salmon for jam butties. (*l to r:* Paul, George, student Michael Lloyd, principal Sir Noel Hall, tutor Mr David Stockton, Ringo, John).

Opposite above right: Ringo with Sir Noel Hall.

This page: Around the time of George's 21st birthday, The Beatles taped an appearance for the variety show *Big Night Out.*

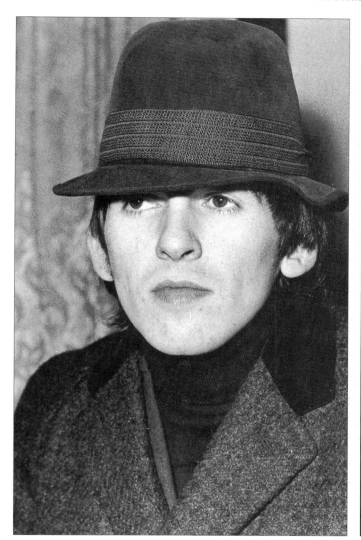

Ringo on set

Ringo on set at 6.00am at the Turk's Head, Twickenham. The film's working title is still *Beatlemania* and thousands of Liverpudlian fans protest that the film should have been made in the group's home town.

Opposite above: Ringo and actress Pattie Boyd in the Turk's Head. The pub is renamed the Liverpool Arms for the film, with a street market to add dockland authenticity.

Opposite above: Paul and George take advantage of Ringo's early-morning set call (*this page*) by attending a Pickwick Club party for Sammy Davis Jnr. Accompanying them are actresses Hayley Mills and Jane Asher, Paul's new girlfriend.

Opposite below: Paul and Jane chatting to dancer Lionel Blair and comedian Dickie Henderson at the Pickwick Club party.

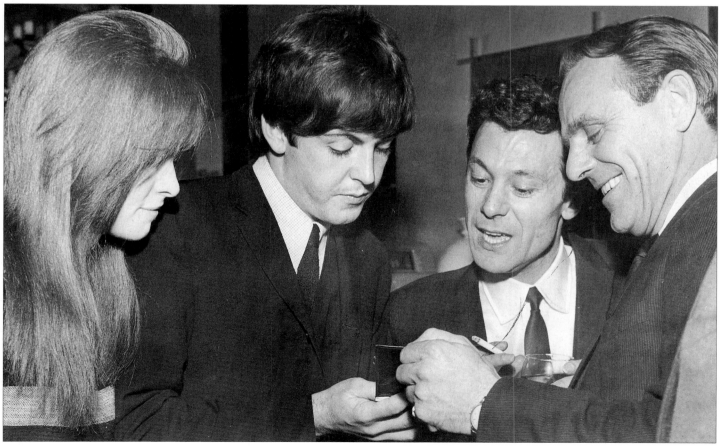

A Hard Day's Night

Right: These four lucky girls not only appear in The Beatles' film as fans, but also get the job of running their combs through the most famous hair in the world. No wonder it's smiles all round from (*l to r*) Pattie Boyd, Tina Williams, Pru Bury and Susan Whiteman.

Below: Paul relaxes at the piano during a break from filming at Twickenham Studios.

Personalities of the year

The Beatles win the Variety Club Show Business Personality of the Year award for 1963. The luncheon ceremony, held at the Dorchester Hotel, is hosted by Opposition leader Harold Wilson.

Opposite: Paul on set at Twickenham.

'The Nation is Proud'

Labour Party Leader Harold Wilson presented the awards during the Variety Club Luncheon at the Dorchester Hotel on 19 March: 'I will refrain from making political capital out of The Beatles...we are all proud of the creation of a new musical idiom in the world of communications.'

Wilson takes a sideswipe at Prime Minister Sir Alec Douglas-Home's recent comments regarding The Beatles as a valuable export commodity for Britain.

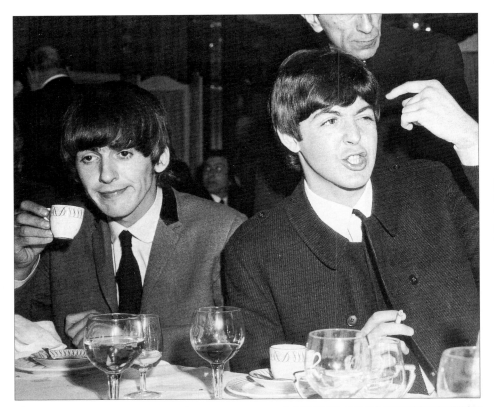

Thumbs up and a speech from George as
the group of the year celebrate their award.

John enjoys a nice cup of tea with Mary Wilson as the celebrations continue at the Variety Club awards luncheon.

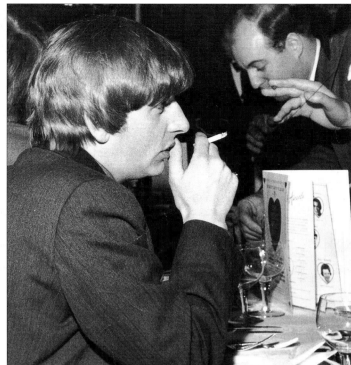

Ready, Steady, Go!

March 20 is Beatles night on television. The group perform live on ATV's *Ready, Steady, Go!*, with the Variety Club awards ceremony broadcast later the same evening.

Opposite above: The boys put their feet up during a break in filming at the Scala Theatre, while John takes the opportunity to publicize his book. Also pictured is producer Walter Shenson, who had negotiated a three-film deal with Brian Epstein the previous autumn. Shenson, working on behalf of United Artists, was hoping to exploit a loophole in The Beatles' EMI recording contract, which did not cover movie soundtracks. This meant that even if the movie bombed, there would be lucrative album sales to make up for it.

Opposite below: The Duke of Edinburgh presents the Carl-Alan awards at the Empire Ballroom, Leicester Square. The Beatles win two awards: Best Group of 1963, and Best Vocal Record, for 'She Loves You'.

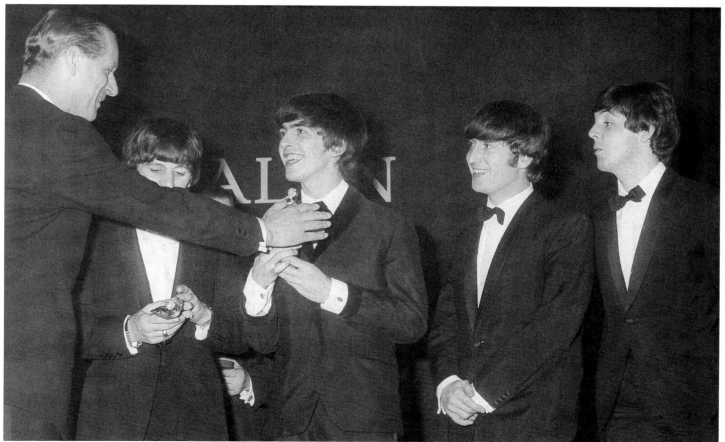

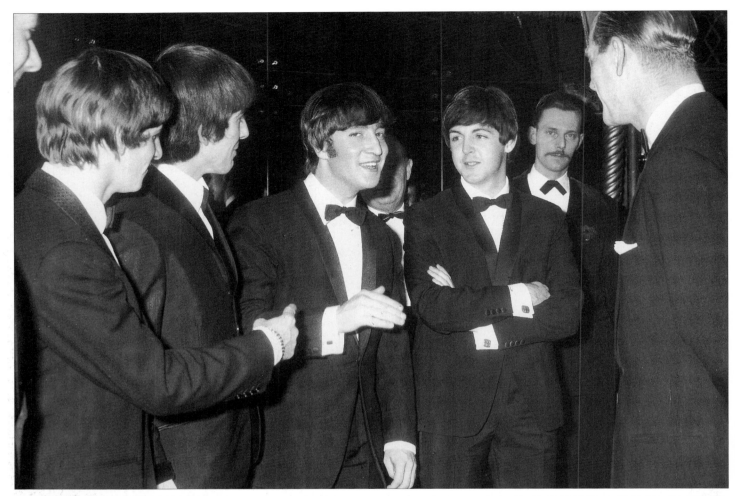

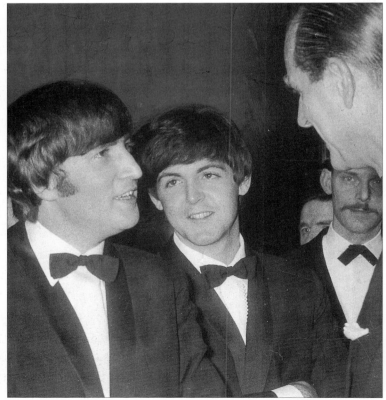

I'm happy just to dance with you...

MP Bessie Braddock gets a close-up view of what the Prime Minister calls 'our best exports'.

Opposite: Paul celebrates their latest honour with a Havana cigar. There's little time for resting on laurels, however. The following day sees the release of 'Can't Buy Me Love', which goes straight to No 1 on both sides of the Atlantic. Hardly surprising, as advance orders had been a world-record three million.

Ringo has a strum and a smoke when not required on set at the Scala Theatre, where the performance scenes for *A Hard Day's Night* were shot. Filming was hindered by a dispute over the unpaid extras used for the audience, which was only resolved when the 350 extras were given £3 15 shillings with lunch thrown in. Among their number was a callow youth who would go on to make his own mark in the world of popular music: one Phil Collins.

Opposite: Filming the nightclub scene at the exclusive Les Ambassadeurs Club, London on the 17 April. The change in title from *Beatlemania* to *A Hard Day's Night* is announced in the media.

Below: Relaxing on a train.

Twist and shout

The Beatles assembled at Les Ambassadeurs Club in the afternoon to film the nightclub scene for *A Hard Day's Night*. Ringo is dancing (to 'Twist and Shout') with Maggy London. Paul is in the background (*and opposite*) with Merrill Colebrook.

When asked to comment on the title change from *Beatlemania* to *A Hard Day's Night*, the producer said 'It means something if you don't think about it too much'.

Opposite below: John is guest of honour at a Foyle's literary luncheon on 23 April, his book *In His Own Write* having been published a month earlier. John chats with Lionel Bart but disappoints the audience by declining to make a speech.

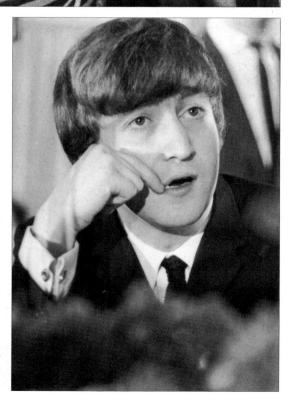

The Beatles and the Bard...

It's the Bard Beatle-style. The boys ham it up in a spoof version of *A Midsummer Night's Dream* for the TV show *Around The Beatles*. The show also featured them playing in their regular performance mode, and it was trailed that they would not be miming to their records. This was taken to equate to a live performance, but Epstein chose his words carefully. He was concerned about how The Beatles sounded on TV, so in this instance the group did indeed mime - but it was to a specially recorded set rather than the actual records.

Right: John at his Foyle's literary lunch.

Welcome to Edinburgh

When The Beatles arrive at Turnhouse airport, Edinburgh, on 29 April for the first of two consecutive nights in Scotland, they are presented with a lucky mascot by one of their young fans, Linda McLean.

Opposite: The concerts, in Edinburgh and in Glasgow, were promoted by Albert Bonici with Brian Epstein and were both hugely successful.

In person - The Beatles

Although a few lucky fans did meet The Beatles in person, the cinema would not hold all those who had applied for tickets so there were hundreds of disappointed people outside just waiting for a glimpse of their idols. The concerts were so successful that The Beatles returned to Scotland in October, playing at Edinburgh, Dundee and Glasgow during their UK tour.

Below and opposite below: Inside, the boys sign autographs and chat to a few of the lucky ones.

PS I Love You

Fame inevitably meant meeting fans and signing endless autographs, which sometimes got The Beatles down, but in Edinburgh they seem to be enjoying all the attention from some of their younger fans.

Just a few beers...

After a disastrous charity reception at the British Embassy in Washington, where The Beatles were pushed around by junior officials and ordered to sign autographs - and where one 'distinguished' guest just walked up and snipped off a lock of Ringo's hair - the boys had refused to attend any more official functions. In Edinburgh, however, the Lord Provost sat down in the bar with them without any formality and a good time was had by all.

Opposite below: John takes a closer look at the heavy gold chain of office sported by the Lord Provost.

On stage at last. The Beatles played one concert in Edinburgh and two at the Glasgow Odeon the following night.

'Which way to the stage?'

Opposite and below: 'I tell you it's not that way!' The boys fool around for the cameras before they take to the stage.

While in Edinburgh, The Beatles also give an interview to BBC Scotland Radio reporter Bill Aitkenhead, which is broadcast that evening on the Scottish Home Service programme *Scottish News*.

Right: Beatlemania Scottish style.

Below right: Autograph production line.

One last photocall and the chance to meet a fan more their own age, then The Beatles are off to Glasgow.

Face to face

Opposite: On 29 April, The Beatles are on hand for the unveiling of their 1963-style effigies at Madame Tussaud's. The waxworks company's profits rocketed in the period following the inclusion of The Beatles.

Below: Julian Lennon around the time of his first birthday. In the early days of Beatlemania, Cynthia conspired with John to conceal the fact that he was both married and a father. On one shopping excursion with Julian, she tried to pass herself off to reporters as her own twin sister. The ridiculous attempt to lie failed, and pictures of Julian in his Silver Cross appeared in next day's papers.

Bottom: George and Pattie returning from holiday just prior to the world tour getting under way.

Right: Paul busy with autographs.

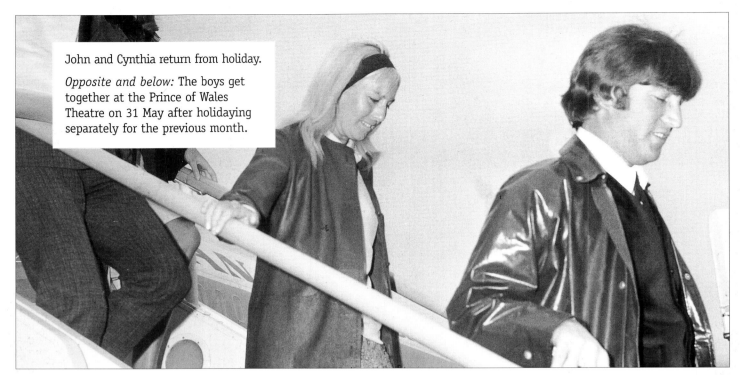

John and Cynthia return from holiday.

Opposite and below: The boys get together at the Prince of Wales Theatre on 31 May after holidaying separately for the previous month.

Around the World

The world tour is announced. The first concert will be held in Copenhagen, Denmark and they will then take in Australia and their first concert tour of America. They also plan five summer performances at British seaside resorts.

Cheers!

The Beatles drink to their forthcoming world tour at a Press conference held at the Prince of Wales Theatre in London.

Opposite bottom: Getting back in the groove; Paul preparing for two performances at the Prince of Wales Theatre.

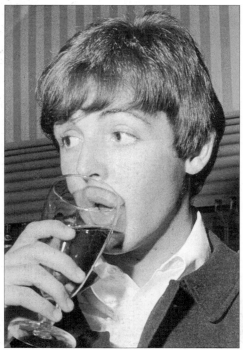

The Beatles seemed to find themselves behind the bar for celebratory drinks on a regular basis - later in the year they toast the success of their UK tour, at the Odeon in Leeds.

Opposite below: Ringo puts on a brave face as he is admitted to University College Hospital, having collapsed at a photo-shoot earlier.

Jimmy in the nick of time...

Session drummer Jimmy Nicol gets rather more than 15 minutes of fame when he is called in as a last-minute replacement for Ringo, who is diagnosed as having tonsilitis and pharyngitis. A rehearsal at EMI Studios is hastily arranged, and Nicol gets the nod of approval.

Jimmy basks in the temporary limelight as he flies out to Denmark with John, George and Paul. He had joined Georgie Fame's Blue Flames only the week before, but this part-tour would represent the pinnacle of his musical achievement. When Ringo rejoins the group in Australia, Nicol receives £500 and a gold watch before returning to relative obscurity.

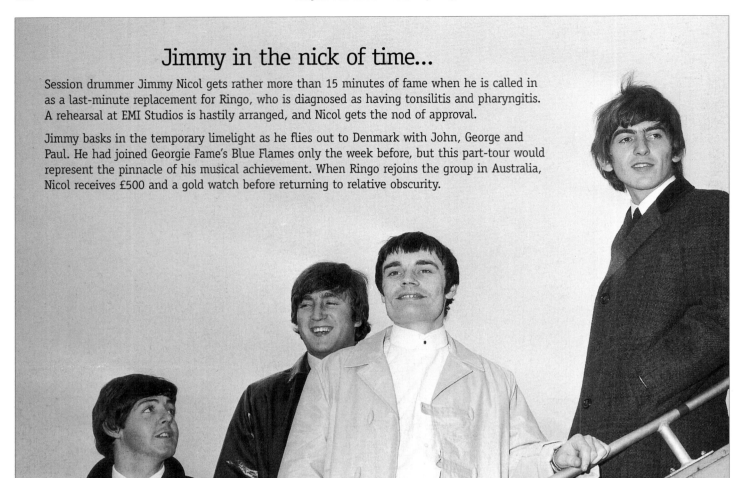

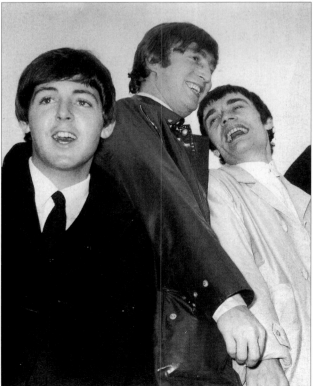

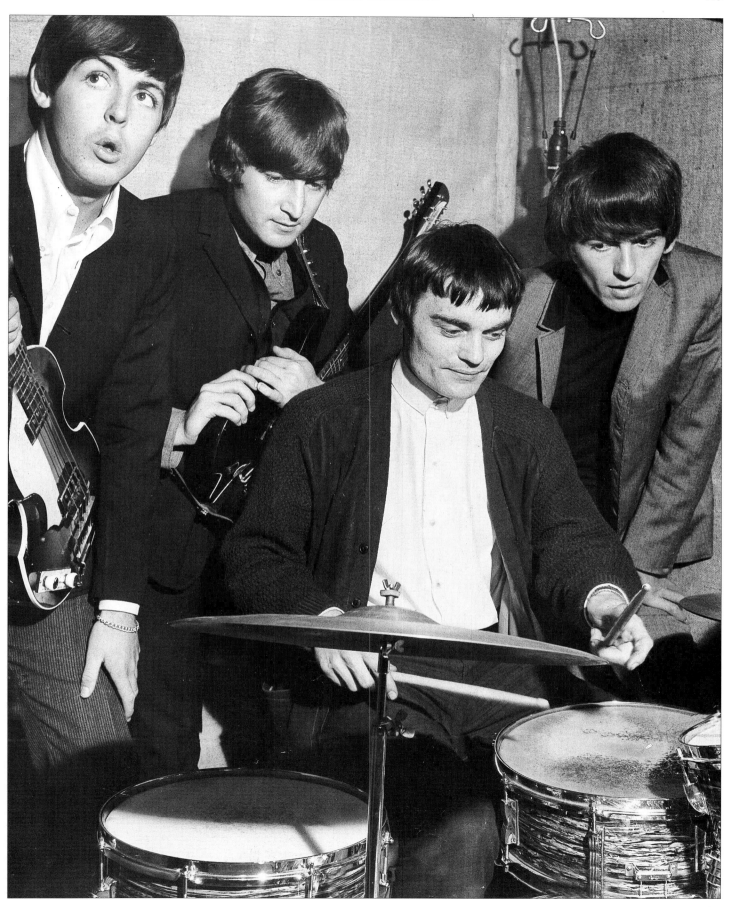

The world at their feet

Paul shows off a pair of clogs, a souvenir from the Dutch leg of the world tour.

Opposite above: The Beatles down under. The boys acknowledge their Australian fans from their 8th-floor suite in a Sydney hotel.

Opposite below: Beatle boards plane with Scarlett woman. The shot makes it look as though they are an item, but it is merely a coincidence that actress Vivien Leigh is catching the same flight for Australia as Ringo.

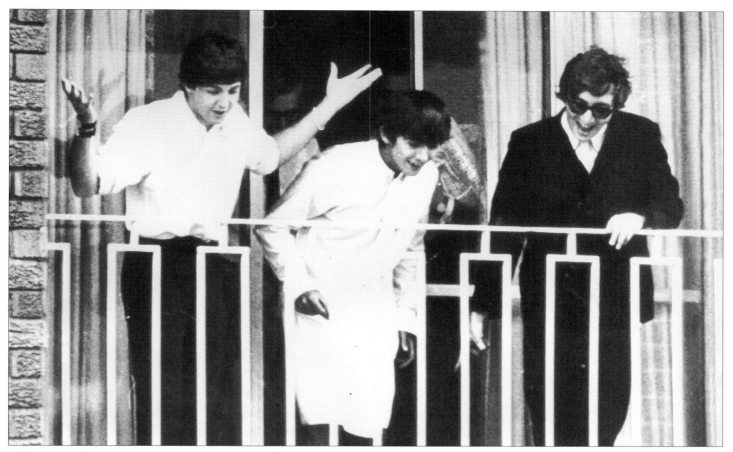

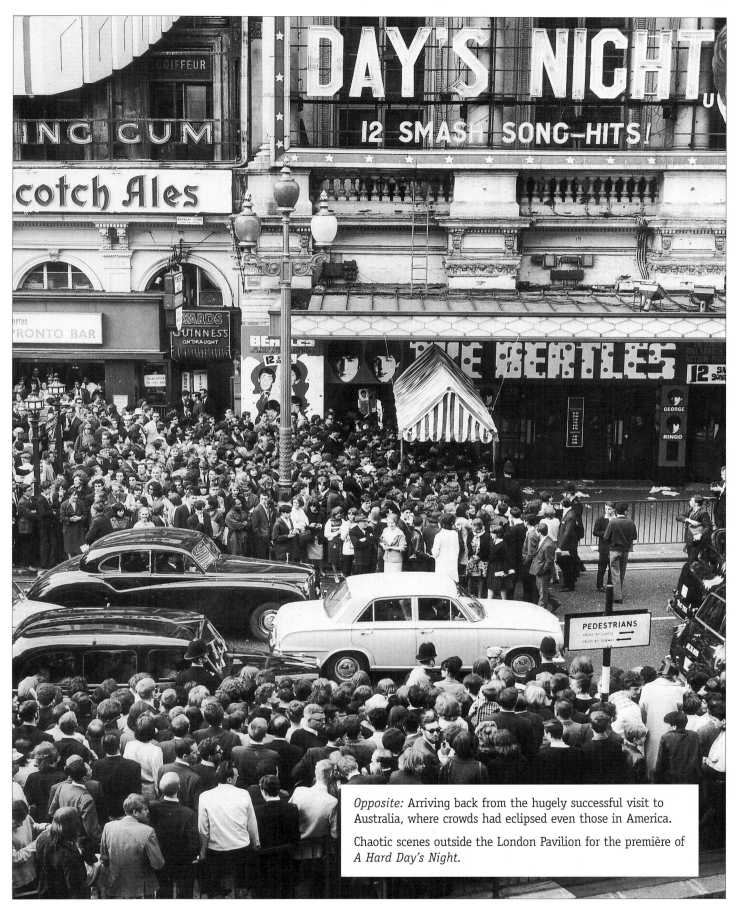

Opposite: Arriving back from the hugely successful visit to Australia, where crowds had eclipsed even those in America.

Chaotic scenes outside the London Pavilion for the première of *A Hard Day's Night*.

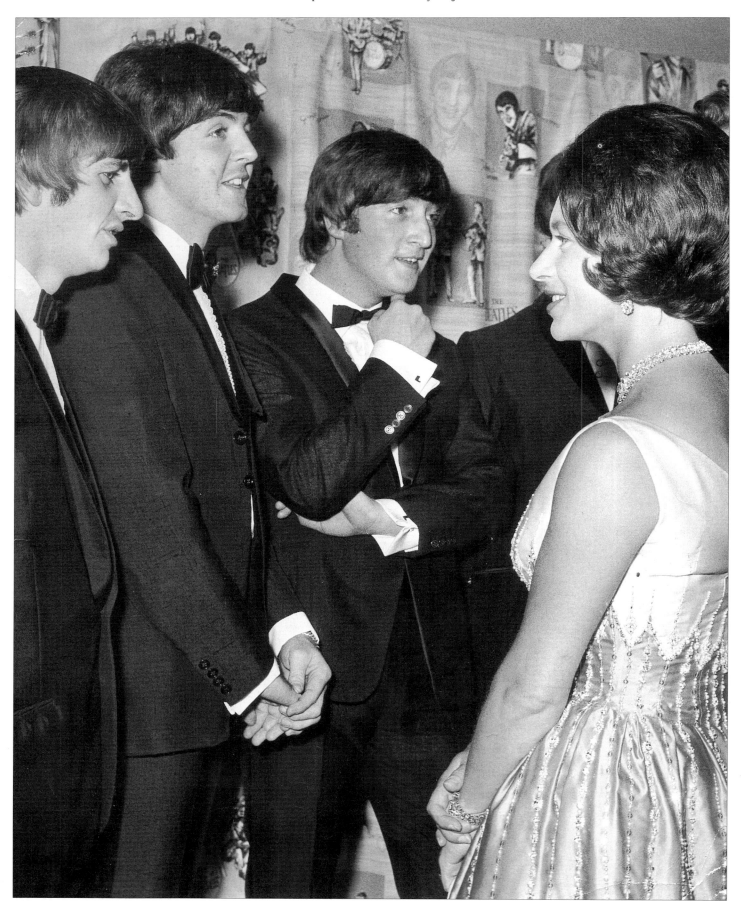

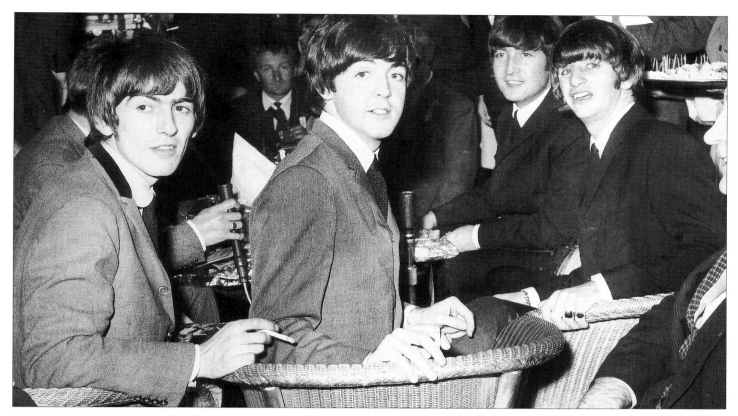

Liverpool lads

Opposite: Princess Margaret meets the group at the première of *A Hard Day's Night* at the London Pavilion. The LP of the same name was released a couple of weeks later and went to the top of the charts. It was the first Beatles album to feature exclusively Lennon/McCartney compositions.

Above: Liverpool honours its four favourite sons. The Beatles are given a civic reception at the Town Hall, having attended the northern première of *A Hard Day's Night*.

Right: Paul at the ABC Theatre, Blackpool.

Live in Blackpool

The Beatles appear in the live variety programme *Blackpool Night Out*, which is hosted by Mike and Bernie Winters. As well as performing some of their songs, they also appear in several comedy sketches.

Hail the conquering heroes

Having taken America by storm on their first proper US tour, a few fans think that Paul's talents would not go amiss in Parliament.

Above: Brian Epstein looks on as The Beatles wave the fans goodbye at New York's Kennedy Airport. The tour had taken in 24 cities over 34 days, with the boys playing 32 concerts. Kansas City was not part of the schedule, but a local businessman persuaded them to play a 35-minute set there for a record fee of $150,000.

Opposite: On stage in Dundee, during the Scottish leg of their UK tour.

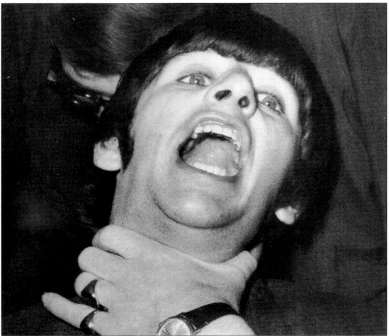

I Feel Fine

Left: Ringo lets the world have a last look at some of the most celebrated tonsils in the world. He books into University College Hospital to have them removed.

Above: Patience with the patient. George kills time with Ringo, playing the Chinese version of the game.

Ringo leaves hospital after a week, humming the latest Beatles' No 1: 'I Feel Fine'. Just in case any ultra-determined fan has any designs on a rather exclusive, if ghoulish, piece of Beatles' memorabilia, he announces that the tonsils in question have been burned.

Opposite: Far out, man. That's The Beatles' view of Eskimo-land, which seems to them to be one of the few places they haven't visited in 1964. They deck themselves out in the appropriate gear instead, for their Christmas show at the Hammersmith Odeon.

Chapter Three

1965

Eight Days A Week

This year was really just more of the same for The Beatles. They released three singles, three EPs and two LPs and made a second film, *Help!*, a comic-strip adventure about the attempts of an obscure Middle-Eastern sect to recover a sacred sacrificial ring that a fan had sent to Ringo. This offered opportunities for location filming, so scenes in the Bahamas and Austria were written into the storyline. But the boys soon became bored during the long hours filming and turned to smoking pot to fill the time, so their concentration was not one hundred percent. Despite this, the film was shot in under three months and was released within a further two months. It did good business and was well received by the critics.

Apart from filming and recording, the group's life was still dominated by touring, with a European tour to France, Italy and Spain, another tour across America and finally a short tour around Britain. All four Beatles had begun to feel that this relentless touring with its suffocating adulation was becoming almost impossible to bear. They were now subject to death threats and the unintentional terrorization by fans was getting even more out of hand. In Houston, Texas, at 2.00 am in the morning, 5000 screaming teenagers broke through the airport barriers and a police cordon and were soon thronging round the plane, climbing on to the wings to peer through the windows and catch a glimpse of their idols. The Beatles were trapped and the pilot was unable to taxi the plane to safety as the fans were underneath it and around the wheels. The boys finally managed to escape through an emergency exit into a service truck and make their getaway.

During concerts John now quite regularly told the fans to 'Shaddup!', and they discovered that even if one of them stopped playing for a few seconds no one noticed. Their music had suffered because of the impossibility of playing well under such conditions; they had once been proud of the fact that they were a tight group of accomplished musicians, but now hardly bothered to rehearse before a tour and often ended up playing abysmally at concerts. Who could blame them when everything was totally inaudible and no one seemed to be interested in listening anyway?

As they became increasingly angered by the mayhem around them, they began to turn their attention to pleasing themselves rather than their public. It was no longer possible to develop new songs on tour as they had in the old days, so they turned more to the recording studio and to working on a progressive complexity of sound. They told Brian Epstein that they wanted to give up touring, and vetoed his suggestions of another *Royal Command Performance* and another Christmas show. He managed to talk them into one more short tour of Britain that winter, which became the last that they ever did in the UK.

This was also the year in which The Beatles received their MBEs. The announcement was received with disbelief – not only by some of the battle-scarred previous recipients who returned their awards in disgust, but also by the group themselves. They assumed they had been honoured for their services to the British export industry, rather than for playing rock music, but even so no pop artiste had been received such an award before. There was some talk initially about turning the honour down, as they all felt that it was too 'Establishment', but in the end they accepted it.

On a personal note, by now each of them was settled with a partner. John and Cynthia had been married since 1962 and had a two-year-old son, while Ringo had married Maureen at the beginning of 1965 and their first son had just been born. Paul had been seeing actress Jane Asher since 1963 and George was living with model Pattie Boyd, whom he had met on the set of *A Hard Day's Night* in 1964. Although this didn't seem to affect the group's popularity, during the height of Beatlemania the wives and girlfriends were quite often subjected to abuse and attack from hysterical fans who were convinced that they alone were destined to be with their chosen Beatle.

But Beatlemania was finally beginning to show signs of running out of steam. In 1965, for the first time, some of the concert venues were not full to capacity and far fewer fans turned up at the airports to welcome the group or wave them a fond farewell. There were still plenty of fans, but perhaps they had begun to realize that it was a waste of money to pay for seats at a concert where their heroes could be as much as 500 yards away and at which they could not hear a note of the music. But The Beatles were still amazingly popular – as Newcastle University's Professor Strang said at the time, 'You can walk down any street of the most primitive village in a country where no one speaks English and hear children chanting the words of the latest Beatles hit'.

Below: George inspects his MBE.
Previous page: The Beatles in the Bahamas filming *Help!*.

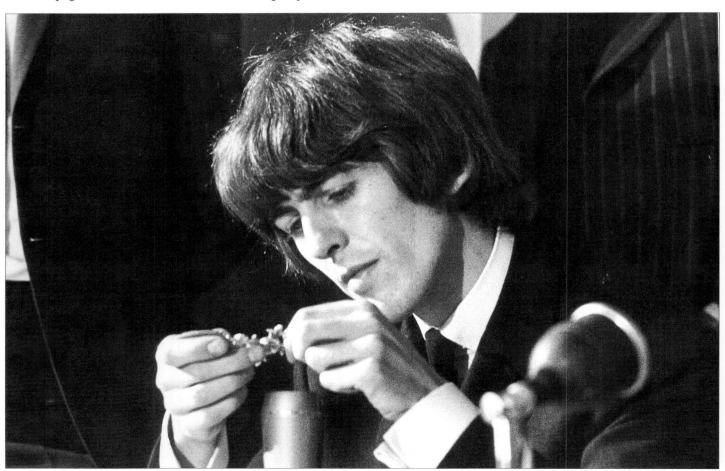

1965: Chronology

11 February	Ringo marries Mary (Maureen) Cox
12 February	The newly-married couple hold a Press conference at the beginning of their honeymoon in Hove, East Sussex
15 February	A single, 'Eight Days a Week'/'I Don't Want to Spoil the Party', is released in the US
22 February	The Beatles fly to the Bahamas to begin shooting their second film, *Help!*
13 March	After a couple of days in Britain, The Beatles fly to Austria, for more location filming
22 March	An LP, *The Early Beatles*, is released in the US
6 April	The EP *Beatles For Sale* is released in the UK
9 April	The single, 'Ticket To Ride'/'Yes It Is', is released in the UK (19 April in the US)
14 April	The communal house sequence for *Help!* is filmed in Ailsa Avenue, Twickenham
26 April	Ex-Beatle Pete Best is interviewed in the *Daily Mirror*
3-5 May	A sequence for *Help!* is filmed on Salisbury Plain
20 May	The Beatles record their last-ever music session for BBC radio
4 June	The EP *Beatles For Sale (No 2)* is released in the UK
7 June	The BBC broadcasts the last radio performance, *The Beatles (Invite You To Take A Ticket To Ride)*, which was pre-recorded on 26 May
11 June	At midnight, it is announced that The Beatles are to be awarded MBEs
14 June	An LP, *Beatles VI*, is released in the US
20 June	A short European concert tour of France, Italy and Spain starts with a concert in Paris
1 July	John's second book, *A Spaniard in the Works*, is released
19 July	The single, 'Help!'/'I'm Down', is released in the US (23 July in the UK)
29 July	*Help!* has its royal world charity première at the London Pavilion
1 August	The Beatles play live on ITV's *Blackpool Night Out*
6 August	The LP *Help!* is released in the UK (13 August in the US)
15 August	The Beatles open their second US tour with a landmark concert at New York's Shea Stadium, witnessed by a then-record audience of 55,600
27 August	The Beatles meet Elvis Presley at his Beverly Hills home on Perugia Way
13 September	Ringo and Maureen Starkey have a son, Zak
13 September	A single, 'Yesterday'/'Act Naturally', is released in the US
26 October	The Beatles receive their MBEs from the Queen in the Great Throne Room at Buckingham Palace
3 December	The Beatles start their last UK tour, playing at the Odeon Cinema, Glasgow
3 December	The single, 'We Can Work It Out'/'Day Tripper', is released in the UK (6 December in the US)
3 December	The LP *Rubber Soul* is released in the UK (6 December in the US)
6 December	The EP *The Beatles' Million Sellers* is released in the UK
17 December	ITV broadcasts *The Music of Lennon & McCartney* around Britain, except in London where it had already been transmitted the previous evening

Testing time

No more 'watching the wheels' for John as he passes his driving test at the age of 24. He receives his congratulations in the EMI Studios car park, at the wheel of George Martin's car.

Fallen idol

John parts company with one of his skis during a lesson at St Moritz. In fact, John proved quite adept on the slopes, staging the spill purely for the benefit of impatient cameramen.

Opposite: Ringo and his new bride, 18-year-old former hairdresser Maureen Cox, pose for the cameras at Hove, Sussex, where they are honeymooning at a house owned by Beatles solicitor David Jacobs. The couple had married the previous day at Caxton Hall Register Office in London - at 8.00 am to avoid the fans.

Help!

The Beatles are given a rapturous send-off at London Airport as they leave for the Bahamas, where shooting of their second film is to begin.

Eight arms to hold you...

Above: Actress Eleanor Bron is the envy of hordes of screaming teenage girls as she flies out to the Bahamas with The Beatles to co-star in *Help!*. A leading light in the satirical comedy fringe, 26-year-old Miss Bron would not have experienced anything like the mass hysteria and adulation which accompanies the Fab Four.

Right and opposite: Cooling off in the Bahamas. The project went through several working titles, including *Eight Arms To Hold You*, before director Dick Lester came up with *Help!*.

Hot stuff

It's bikini weather in the Bahamas, and Paul (*opposite*) finds it hard to keep his eyes on the road.

Paul and George pictured at London
Airport, a couple of weeks into the 11-week
shooting schedule for *Help!*.

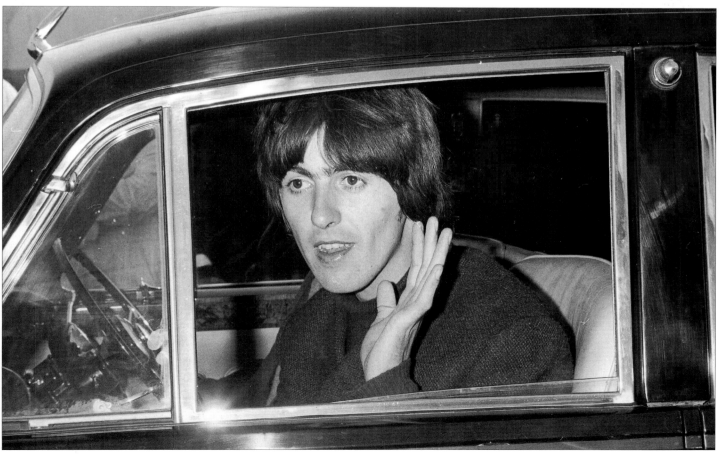

Paul takes to the slopes

Paul takes advantage of location filming in Austria to try his hand at skiing. His instructor is Harriet Davidson, niece of the Duke of Norfolk.

Opposite above: Radio Caroline DJ Simon Dee presents the pirate station's First Birthday 'Bell' Award to The Beatles at Twickenham Film Studios.

Opposite below: The Mersey Sound hits Salisbury Plain. Filming on a chilly May afternoon, with a backdrop of Army personnel on manoeuvres. Army sergeant Douglas Gunn looks askance at two mop-tops.

John and Eleanor Bron on location in Ailsa Avenue, Twickenham.
Opposite and overleaf: Ringo does his best to keep warm between takes.

Off to check out the competition. Having completed filming on
Help! a few days earlier, John flies out to the Cannes Film Festival,
accompanied by Cynthia.

Birthday honours

The calm before the storm. Paul gives the thumbs up as The Beatles become the first pop group to feature in the honours list. Many were astonished and angered by the news, however, regarding it as a debasement of the award. Behind the scenes, even the members of the group themselves had reservations about whether to accept.

Opposite: Paul reads all about it as he returns from a holiday with Jane Asher in Albufeira, Portugal.

Paul, with Jane Asher. Speculation was rife that they were about to marry - or had done so already in secret.
Opposite: Paul on his 23rd birthday is carried aloft.

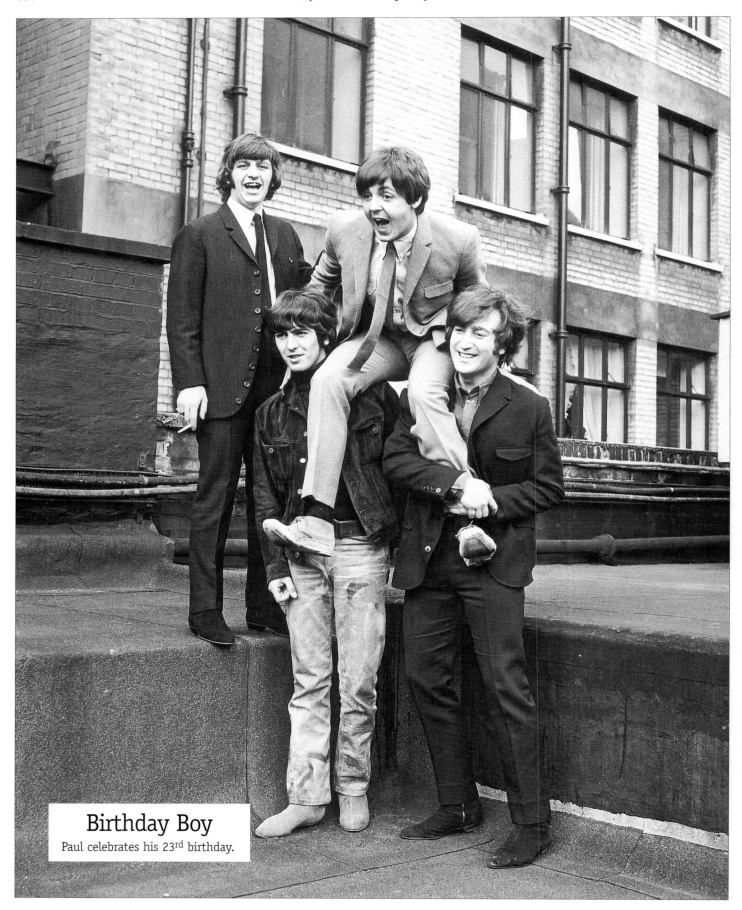

Birthday Boy
Paul celebrates his 23rd birthday.

Help!

The Beatles in formal attire on the occasion of the royal charity première of *Help!* at the London Pavilion. 'We'd be much happier in jeans and T-shirts,' said George. Also pictured are Cynthia Lennon and Maureen Starr.

Drummer's boy.

Above and previous page: John, Paul, George and
Ringo acknowledge their fans as they return home
from their second US tour. A few days earlier the idols
had met their own idol - Elvis - at his Beverly Hills
home in Perugia Way, but it was not to prove an
enduring friendship.

Right and opposite: News that Maureen Starr has given
birth to a boy brings the press out in droves to Queen
Charlotte's Hospital, Hammersmith. 'He's about that
big,' (opposite above left) the proud father reveals.
Ringo is more specific about the baby's weight - 8lb -
and announces that the new arrival will be called Zak.

Off to the Palace...

Paul and Ringo head off to the Palace from Ringo's house in Montagu Square. Tradition favours top hat and tails on such occasions, but The Beatles opt for dark lounge suits to collect their MBEs.

Opposite above: Leaving a besieged Buckingham Palace.

Opposite below: The four show off their medals, following their investiture.

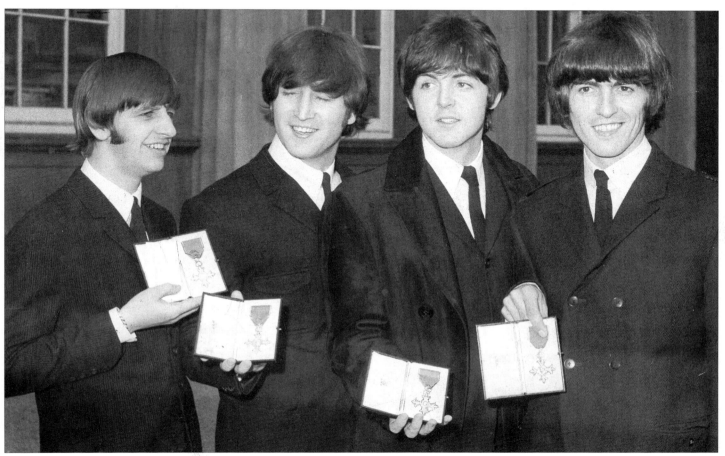

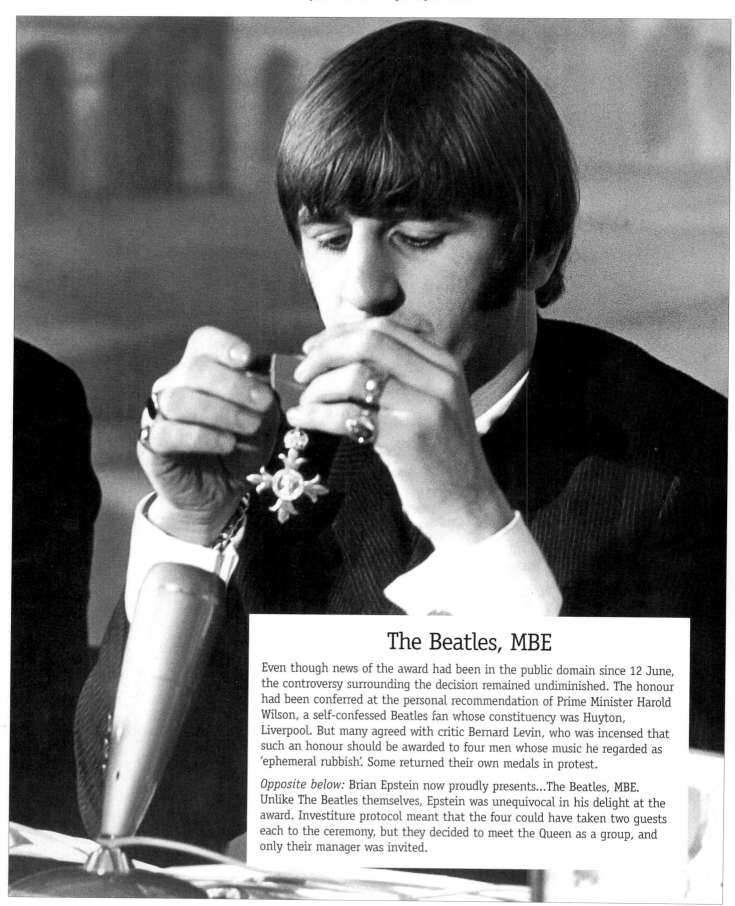

The Beatles, MBE

Even though news of the award had been in the public domain since 12 June, the controversy surrounding the decision remained undiminished. The honour had been conferred at the personal recommendation of Prime Minister Harold Wilson, a self-confessed Beatles fan whose constituency was Huyton, Liverpool. But many agreed with critic Bernard Levin, who was incensed that such an honour should be awarded to four men whose music he regarded as 'ephemeral rubbish'. Some returned their own medals in protest.

Opposite below: Brian Epstein now proudly presents...The Beatles, MBE. Unlike The Beatles themselves, Epstein was unequivocal in his delight at the award. Investiture protocol meant that the four could have taken two guests each to the ceremony, but they decided to meet the Queen as a group, and only their manager was invited.

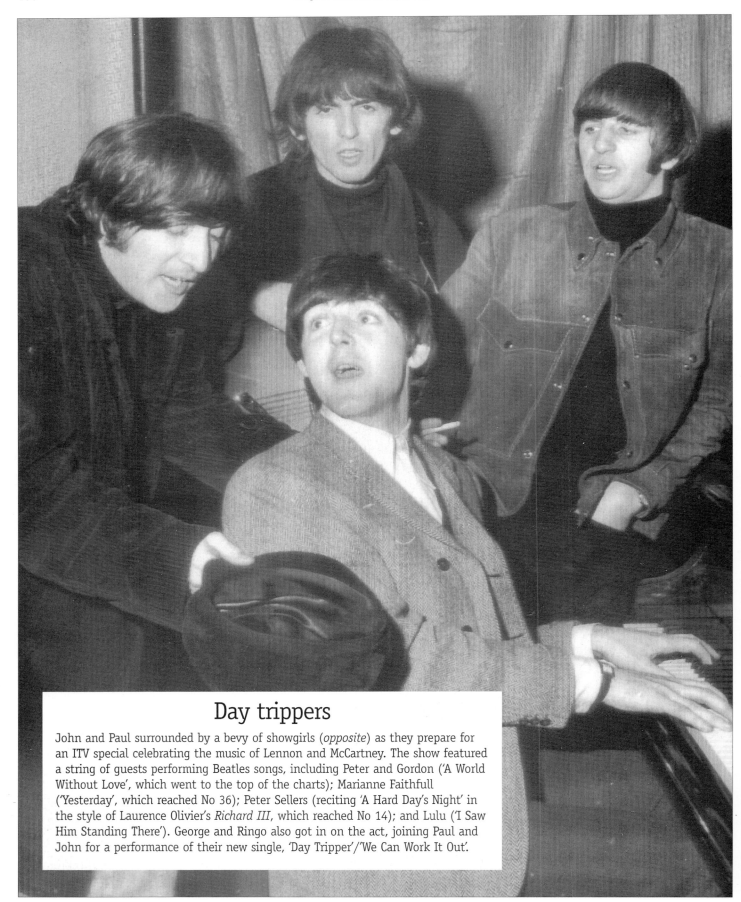

Day trippers

John and Paul surrounded by a bevy of showgirls (*opposite*) as they prepare for an ITV special celebrating the music of Lennon and McCartney. The show featured a string of guests performing Beatles songs, including Peter and Gordon ('A World Without Love', which went to the top of the charts); Marianne Faithfull ('Yesterday', which reached No 36); Peter Sellers (reciting 'A Hard Day's Night' in the style of Laurence Olivier's *Richard III*, which reached No 14); and Lulu ('I Saw Him Standing There'). George and Ringo also got in on the act, joining Paul and John for a performance of their new single, 'Day Tripper'/'We Can Work It Out'.

Chapter Four

1966

Hello Goodbye

lthough The Beatles had decided that they wanted to stop touring, as yet there had been no definite decision to quit so at first everyone expected 1966 to follow much the same format as the previous year. They did take a four-month break from live performances, using the time to work in the recording studio, but then a series of disasters turned the year into a nightmare for the band.

In March, the group had their official publicity photographs taken by Robert Whittaker. They were dressed normally in sweaters and dark jackets, but for some reason others were also taken with them all dressed up in butcher's white coats and posing with lumps of meat and dismembered dolls. One of these pictures was used in Britain to promote their new single, 'Paperback Writer', without apparent comment, but the shot was also used for the cover of a new LP, *Yesterday And Today*, released by Capitol in America. When advance copies went out in mid-June and the photo started to appear on advertising billboards, there was an immediate outcry about its offensive nature. Capitol had to recall all copies and replace the picture with one showing the band standing round a suitcase, all of which cost them a fortune.

In the middle of this, The Beatles set out on a tour of West Germany, Japan and the Philippines. The tour started well and

they were warmly welcomed when they arrived in Hamburg after an absence of three years, but things began to go badly wrong on the way to Tokyo. First their flight was diverted because of a typhoon and had to touch down in Alaska for several hours. When The Beatles finally arrived in Japan they found themselves facing another storm: the local promoter had booked the Nippon Budokan, a magnificent hall that until then had been dedicated to traditional Japanese martial arts. Many Japanese considered it to be a sacred building and were horrified that it was to be used for Western pop music, with its screaming fans. Opposition to the concerts was bitter and there were angry demonstrations and marches. The police were out in force and each concert had 3000 officers strategically placed among the fans, ready to quell any pandemonium. As a result, 10,000 fans sat quietly to listen to the music - but by this time the band's level of musicianship had slipped so far that almost everything was mistimed and off-key.

The police also mounted an armed guard on the group's hotel, and they were forbidden to step outside. When they tried to slip out to view Tokyo, they were swiftly rounded up and returned to their rooms. John did escape briefly, but the security force then threatened to withdraw completely. If this was bad, things were to get much worse on their next stop in the Philippines.

Ferdinand and Imelda Marcos were at the height of their dictatorship when The Beatles arrived in Manila. The president, his wife and their three children were invited as guests of honour to the concerts and local papers reported that the band would be paying a courtesy call at the palace at 11.00 am. The boys were apparently not aware they were expected and didn't appear. They performed their two concerts, but the following morning the newspapers were full of stories about Imelda being 'stood up', the British Embassy and The Beatles themselves received bomb and death threats, and the local promoter was so outraged that he refused to hand over the group's share of gate receipts. Brian Epstein quickly organized a televized apology explaining what had happened, but its transmission was mysteriously disrupted by a burst of static. The Philippine tax office refused to let anyone leave until they paid income tax on the concert revenue - which they still hadn't received - so Brian Epstein had to post a bond of £7000. They all then left for the airport, but their security forces had been withdrawn so they were kicked and jostled leaving the hotel and at the terminal. Minutes after The Beatles had left Philippine soil, President Marcos issued a Press statement confirming that they had not intended to slight the First Lady.

A few weeks later there was yet more bad news. An American magazine had picked up an article in which John talked about religion, and in which he had said that The Beatles were more popular than Jesus. This had caused no comment in Britain at the time, but the American article paraphrased what he said out of context, reporting that he had said The Beatles were greater than Jesus. Within days the Bible Belt was in an uproar, with Beatles merchandise being ceremoniously burned and their music banned on local radio. This was just days before the start of their tour of America, and things became so fraught that it was nearly cancelled.

In the event it did go ahead, starting with a Press conference at which John explained what he had said and apologized. Even so, the band received death threats and when a fire cracker exploded on stage at Memphis each of them was convinced that one of them had been shot. The final show was at Candlestick Park in San Francisco, where The Beatles played until exactly 10.00 pm and then left the stage. The touring was finally over.

Below: A kiss for Pattie from George on their wedding day.
Previous page: The happy couple leaving the register office in Epsom.

1966: Chronology

21 January	George marries Patricia (Pattie) Ann Boyd
8 February	George and Pattie fly to Barbados for their honeymoon
21 February	A single, 'Nowhere Man'/'What Goes On', is released in the US
1 March	A documentary, *The Beatles At Shea Stadium*, which was filmed in 1965 and captures Beatlemania at its peak, is shown on British television
4 March	London's *Evening Standard* newspaper publishes an interview with John in which he states that The Beatles are 'more popular than Jesus now...'
4 March	The EP *Yesterday* is released in the UK
25 March	The infamous 'butcher' photos of The Beatles are taken by Robert Whittaker
1 May	The Beatles give their last proper British concert, at Empire Pool, Wembley
21 May	The Beatles are filmed in the grounds of Chiswick House in London for colour promos of 'Paperback Writer'/'Rain'
30 May	The single, 'Paperback Writer'/'Rain', is released in the US (10 June in the UK)
16 June	The Beatles' only appearance on *Top Of The Pops*, performing 'Paperback Writer' and 'Rain'
20 June	An LP, *Yesterday... and Today* is released in the US, the revised version of *Yesterday And Today*, which was recalled because of complaints about the 'butcher' shots on the cover
24 June	The Beatles embark on a short tour, covering Germany, Japan and the Philippines
5 July	The Beatles run into major problems in the Philippines after being accused of snubbing Imelda Marcos

8 July	The EP *Nowhere Man* is released in the UK
29 July	American teen magazine *Datebook* publishes John's *Evening Standard* interview, asserting that he said The Beatles are 'greater' than Jesus.
5 August	The single 'Eleanor Rigby'/'Yellow Submarine' is released in the UK (8 August in the US)
5 August	The LP *Revolver* is released in the UK (8 August in the US)
6 August	Brian Epstein holds a Press conference in New York to explain John's 'Jesus' remarks
11 August	The Beatles fly to Chicago for their final US tour and John, supported by the others, faces the Press to explain and say he is sorry
13 August	Radio station KLUE in Longview, Texas organizes a public 'Beatles bonfire', but the next morning it is wiped off the air when a lightning bolt hits the transmission tower
29 August	The Beatles give their very last concert at San Francisco's Candlestick Park
5 September	John goes to Celle in West Germany to begin filming his part in *How I Won The War*
9 November	John meets Yoko Ono for the first time when he attends a private view of her art exhibition, *Unfinished Paintings and Objects*, at London's Indica Gallery
27 November	John films a sequence for Peter Cook and Dudley Moore's BBC programme, *Not Only...But Also*, which is shown one month later on 26 December
9 December	The LP *A Collection Of Beatles Oldies* is released in the UK only

Any image change in a Beatle is newsworthy, but Ringo, complete with new beard, has no trend-setting thoughts. 'I hate shaving, and while we're on holiday there's no need to,' he says, as he and Maureen fly out to Trinidad. John and Cynthia join them in a mid-January break.

Opposite: George, 22, marries 21-year-old Pattie Boyd at Epsom Register Office. It was Pattie's resemblance to Brigitte Bardot that first caught George's eye on the set of *A Hard Day's Night*, in which Pattie had a minor part. He had to be persistent, though - she was already engaged to somebody else at the time.

A kiss for the bride

Pattie's red fox fur coat, by Mary Quant, is a wedding present from George; her gift to him is a set of George III wine goblets.

Opposite: A kiss for the bride from the Beatles' one remaining bachelor. John and Ringo are still holidaying in the West Indies and send a telegram of congratulations. Not that they were missed by Registrar Leonard Clarke - he admits he is not a fan and can't tell one Beatle from another.

The perfect cook

George has married the perfect cook. That's his mother's opinion anyway. When asked about her cooking Pattie said 'I do enjoy cooking and am wondering what to prepare for George's Sunday meal.' The happy bride revealed that she will continue modelling, but will not be doing as much as she has been.

Opposite below: The newlyweds, with Brian Epstein behind. He shares the best man duties with Paul.

Left and above: Two weeks after their wedding, George and Pattie leave for Barbados. 'More of a holiday than a honeymoon,' says George.

What's it all about...

Paul and Jane Asher arriving at a private preview of her new film, *Alfie*. With them is Jane's brother Peter - of Peter and Gordon fame.

Opposite above: Not quite the fervour of a Beatles gig at the Italian Institue, Belgravia, as composer Luciano Berio introduces his latest work, *Un Omaggio a Dante* (A Homage To Dante). But the audience does include a famous fellow musician sitting attentively in the front row. The reason? Signor Berio specializes in electronic music, and Paul has indicated that the Beatles are experimenting with different sounds on their new album, *Revolver*.

Opposite below: Paul and Jane Asher arriving at the Plaza Cinema, Haymarket, London, for the première of *Alfie*.

Last British Concert

The Beatles give what is to be their last British concert, at Empire Pool, Wembley on 1 May. A British tour had been pencilled in for the end of the year, but this was eventually shelved, leaving the NME Poll Winners concert as the group's swan song for their home fans. It was a 15-minute, 5-song set: 'I Feel Fine', 'Nowhere Man', 'Day Tripper', 'If I Needed Someone' and 'I'm Down'. Although cameras were present, they stopped rolling for The Beatles' numbers because of a contractual dispute, so no footage exists of this milestone event.

Left: The Beatles rehearsing at BBC Television Centre for what was their only appearance on *Top of the Pops*. They perform the new single, 'Paperback Writer', and the B-side, 'Rain', which had been released six days earlier. Both songs had innovative features. As far as 'Paperback Writer' was concerned, it was neither a love song nor a dance number, and featured Paul playing what amounted to lead bass. On 'Rain' there was the distinctive sound of the backwards guitar. Some critics thought the group's bubble had burst, but the fans still made the single their tenth No 1 success.

Back to Germany

The Beatles leave for a four-day tour of Germany, their first visit to the country since the final trip to Hamburg in December 1962.

Tokyo

After Germany The Beatles fly to Tokyo, where they perform at the Budokan Hall. The authorities went to great lengths to confine Beatlemania to the concert venue, and even inside the auditorium the fans were strictly marshalled. This made for an unusual situation at a Beatles concert: the band could actually be heard. The flaws in the group's singing and playing - the result of several years of deafening noise drowning out the music - were exposed on this occasion. Whether the fans noticed or cared is another matter.

Facing the music

The group arrive back in London and hold a Press conference, following their fraught trip to the Far East. If the Japan leg of the tour had had its difficulties, they were as nothing compared with what was to come in the Philippines. A mix-up meant the four missed an appointment to meet the country's First Lady, Imelda Marcos. This was taken as a direct snub, and The Beatles found themselves in the extraordinary situation of being the focal point of a country's vitriol instead of hero-worship. They and their entourage were involved in some ugly scenes of intimidation and assault before managing to get airborne.

Opposite below: Come home soon; the message from their faithful fans as The Beatles fly off to the United States.

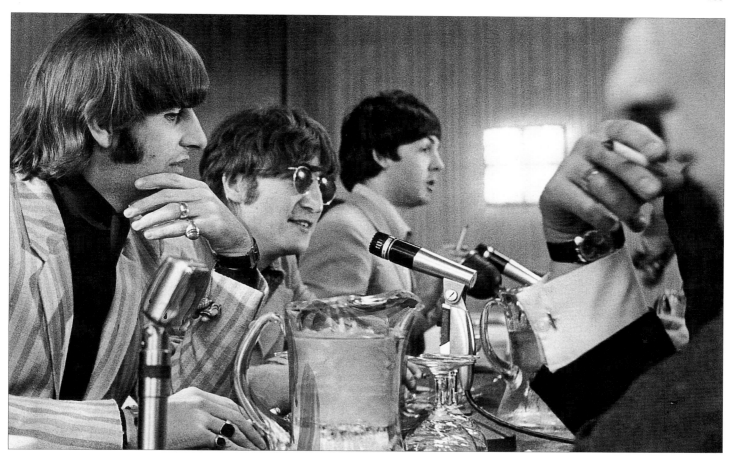

The show is over...

Below: There is a delay in the flight which is to take the group to the United States for their final tour. To kill time they are shown round the new police station at London Airport.

The flight finally gets away, with the usual rousing accompaniment. The reception at the other end is less certain, as John's remarks on the relative popularity of The Beatles and Jesus are rehashed and misquoted. Bonfires are held to burn Beatles records and merchandise, before John eats a little humble pie and manages to smooth things over. In Canada, meanwhile, John has at least one ally in the shape of the Bishop of Montreal, the Rt Rev. Kenneth Maguire, who said: 'I wouldn't be surprised if The Beatles actually were more popular than Jesus. In the only popularity poll in Jesus's time he came out second best to Barabbas.'

But the show is over - the fans don't realize it yet, but John, Paul, George and Ringo knew this was the end of the line as far as touring and concert performance was concerned.

How I Won the War

Just five days after returning from the final US tour, John heads off to Germany for location shooting in Dick Lester's black comedy *How I Won The War*. John has his hair shorn and dons NHS spectacles for his role as Private Gripweed.

Below: Paul and Ringo, pictured with Dusty Springfield and Tom Jones at the *Melody Maker* Awards ceremony, held at the top of the GPO Tower, London.

Opposite: George at London Airport to meet sitar virtuoso Ravi Shankar, who has been teaching him to play the instrument. George was immersing himself more and more in Indian culture, philosophy and religion, as well as music, and had just returned from a five-week visit to the country. He was also keen to introduce the sitar into Beatles music, and it had already featured on their albums *Rubber Soul* and *Revolver*.

Opposite below right: Paul's new 'Viva Zapata' moustache (as it is soon dubbed in the Press) attracts the attention of photographers. He is pictured here returning from a holiday in Kenya. More interesting, perhaps, is the fact that the moustache would survive until 30 March 1967 - the day the famous *Sgt Pepper* album cover is shot - but it has disappeared by the time of this seminal album's release.

Not only ...But Also

The Beatles are in the middle of recording 'Strawberry Fields Forever', when John makes a guest appearance in a sketch for the Peter Cook and Dudley Moore Christmas show, *Not Only...But Also*. John plays the commissionaire of a 'members only' gents lavatory. The outside shots were filmed in Broadwick St, London W1.

Chapter Five

1967

Magical Mystery Tour

With no more touring to be done, The Beatles now needed to find a new focus for their lives. On the business front the group had formed The Beatles & Co, a legal partnership to handle all their business affairs that bound them together until 1977, but on a personal level each was looking in a different direction. George was already interested in India and its religions and music, and his passion for this grew and developed throughout the year. Ringo, who was always perhaps more home-loving than the others, began to spend extra time with his family. John tried acting, but decided he didn't like it or the company of most actors. Paul wrote some music for a film and tried a bit of painting.

Despite these different interests, they still wanted to be together to make music so they turned to the recording studio in earnest, working on their next LP, *Sgt Pepper's Lonely Hearts Club Band*. For some time they had all been experimenting with drugs, including LSD, which had a marked effect on their songwriting - in particular on John's work. The Lennon/McCartney partnership was now no longer really a partnership at all, as each was developing his skill in a different way; John was becoming rather introspective and wrote psychedelic and rather disorientating lyrics, while Paul's songs were much more bright and breezy.

The drugs also had another unexpected side-effect. Until now The Beatles public 'loveable mop-top' image had more or less survived against the odds, but 'A Day In The Life' from *Sgt Pepper* was the first Beatles song to be banned by the BBC, because of its supposed drug references. A couple of days later, when Paul admitted in the newspapers and on television that he had taken LSD, journalists jumped to condemn him. The band's stand on drugs was confirmed when all four Beatles, as well as Brian Epstein, signed a petition published in *The Times* calling for the legalization of marijuana. All this may have disgraced them in the eyes of parents and journalists, but to The Beatles' own generation it just added to their credibility.

But The Beatles themselves were still searching for the Meaning of Life and - having already decided that they were not the answer - had begun to give up drugs. It was at this point that they were introduced to the Maharishi Mahesh Yogi during his visit to London, by George's wife, Pattie. They all initially thought they had found what they were looking for, and threw themselves behind his movement. All four Beatles, as well as many other major pop stars, followed the Maharishi to Bangor in Wales to study transcendental meditation. The Press initially thought this was some sort of publicity stunt, but The Beatles soon made it clear that they were in earnest.

While they were in Wales, the news came of Brian Epstein's accidental death from an overdose of sleeping tablets. He was apparently rich, successful and happy, but behind the public façade he had felt increasingly lost and depressed after The Beatles gave up touring, since they no longer needed him as much. Despite their rather laid-back public response to the news, they were all devastated. John, in particular, felt that without a manager to lead and organize them, they were finished. At an emergency meeting held at Paul's house days after Brian's death, they discussed their future. Paul suggested they should try to cope by starting work on a project that had been postponed for some time: the filming of the *Magical Mystery Tour*.

The basis of this project was that they should all pile into a bus with a film crew and various other passengers, and just drive round England filming the adventures they were sure to have. There was no firm script, no experienced director and no one had any idea what they were doing. They spent a week driving round Cornwall, Devon and the South of England,

followed by photographers and journalists and causing chaos wherever they went, and a further week at West Malling Air Station – since no one had thought to book Shepperton Studios. The resulting ten hours of film, which took eleven weeks to edit down into the final one-hour version, was shown on BBC television at Christmas and was savagely criticized. The only good news was the music, six new songs written for the film that were also issued on a pair of EPs in a gatefold sleeve, with a 24-page booklet telling the story in photographs.

Perhaps the critics at the time did not make enough allowances for the experimental nature of the film, but by the time it was released The Beatles had moved on anyway. They now saw themselves as businessmen, building an empire in which they would be in total control. The first manifestation of this, the Apple Boutique, opened on Baker Street at the beginning of December.

Below: Paul greets Jane Asher at London Airport.
Previous page: At the photocall for the *Our World* TV broadcast, it is already evident from their different dress styles that each of The Beatles is developing as an individual.

1967: Chronology

6 January	The UK release of *The Family Way*, Paul's soundtrack LP of the music from the film
27 January	A new nine-year recording contract with EMI Records is signed by The Beatles
13 February	The single 'Strawberry Fields Forever'/'Penny Lane' is released in the US (17 February in the UK)
30 March	The famous cover photo for the *Sgt Pepper's Lonely Hearts Club Band* album is shot by Michael Cooper
19 April	A legal business partnership, The Beatles & Co, is formed to bind the group together until 1977
20 April	The first recording session for *Magical Mystery Tour* is held at EMI studios
15 May	While attending a performance by Georgie Fame at the Bag O' Nails Club in London, Paul meets photographer Linda Eastman
19 May	Brian Epstein holds a launch party for *Sgt Pepper's Lonely Hearts Club Band* at his home in London
20 May	The BBC imposes a radio and TV ban on 'A Day In The Life' because of the song's overt drug references
26 May	The LP *Sgt Pepper's Lonely Hearts Club Band* is released in the UK before the official date of 1 June (2 June in the US)
19 June	Paul admits on television that he has taken LSD
24 June	Photo-call and Press conference at Abbey Road studios for the *Our World* TV broadcast
25 June	The Beatles perform 'All You Need Is Love' on the world's first global satellite TV link-up, watched by 400,000,000. It is their last live TV performance
7 July	The single 'All You Need Is Love'/'Baby, You're A Rich Man' is released in the UK (17 July in the US)
24 July	John, Paul, George, Ringo and Brian Epstein lend their names to a petition that is published in *The Times*, calling for the legalization of marijuana
19 August	Ringo and Maureen have a second son, Jason
24 August	John, George and Paul, with wives and friends, attend a lecture by the Maharishi Mahesh Yogi at London's Hilton hotel and become interested in transcendental meditation
25 August	The Beatles and their entourage travel to Bangor, North Wales, to attend a weekend seminar by the Maharishi
27 August	Brian Epstein is found dead in bed at his London home
29 August	Brian Epstein's funeral is held in Liverpool. It is a family affair and is not attended by The Beatles
1 September	The Beatles all meet at Paul's house in St John's Wood to discuss their future
11 September	The Beatles set off in a coach with a camera crew and 43 passengers to begin shooting on their own TV film, *Magical Mystery Tour*
17 October	A memorial service is held for Brian Epstein at the New London Synagogue in Abbey Road
18 October	All The Beatles attend the première of *How I Won The War* at the London Pavilion
24 November	The single 'Hello,Goodbye'/'I Am The Walrus', is released in the UK (27 November in the US)
27 November	The LP *Magical Mystery Tour* is released in the US
3 December	Ringo flies to Rome to begin filming his part in *Candy*
5 December	John and George attend a party heralding the opening of The Beatles' Apple Boutique, two days later
8 December	The EP *Magical Mystery Tour* is released in the UK
25 December	Paul and Jane Asher announce their engagement
26 December	BBC1 transmits the première of *Magical Mystery Tour*
27 December	Paul appears live on *The David Frost Show* to defend *Magical Mystery Tour*

Here We Go Round The Mulberry Bush

Left: Paul and Jane Asher at the première of *Here We Go Round The Mulberry Bush*. Paul had been close to agreeing to write the music for the film, but eventually declined. Steve Winwood's Traffic got the job, and took the film's title song to No 8 in the charts.

Paul with his current car, an Aston Martin. It is during this period, the early part of '67, that he would later admit to experimenting with the 'heaven and hell' drug LSD.

Lonely Hearts Club Band...

Paul pictured at Heathrow after attending Jane Asher's 21st birthday party in Denver, Colorado. Stripes are in, but this is one Beatle moustache that's living on borrowed time.

Opposite: Paul meets Jane Asher at London Airport, following her five-month spell in the United States with the Bristol Old Vic. She would later remark how much changed she had found Paul on her return, citing the fact that she had not shared his experience with LSD.

All You Need is Love

A photo-call at Abbey Road Studios in advance of
the following day's *Our World* satellite broadcast,
in which the group will perform a new song to
400,000,000 people across five continents. For the
sake of the global audience, the brief for the song
is simplicity. John's response is 'All You Need Is
Love', composed just days earlier. The song
receives both critical and popular acclaim, tops
the charts one week after release and becomes
the anthem for the 'summer of love'. The scale of
the *Our World* event is fitting, as it marks The
Beatles' last live television performance.

Below: Paul's Aston Martin affords him little
protection from avid autograph hunters on his
25th birthday.

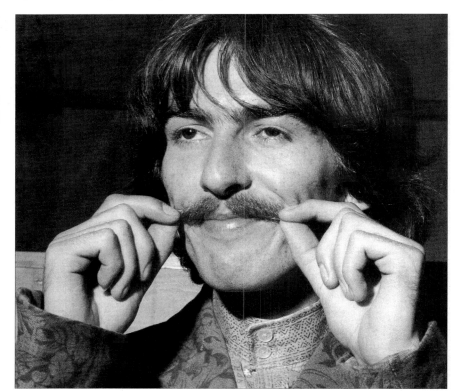

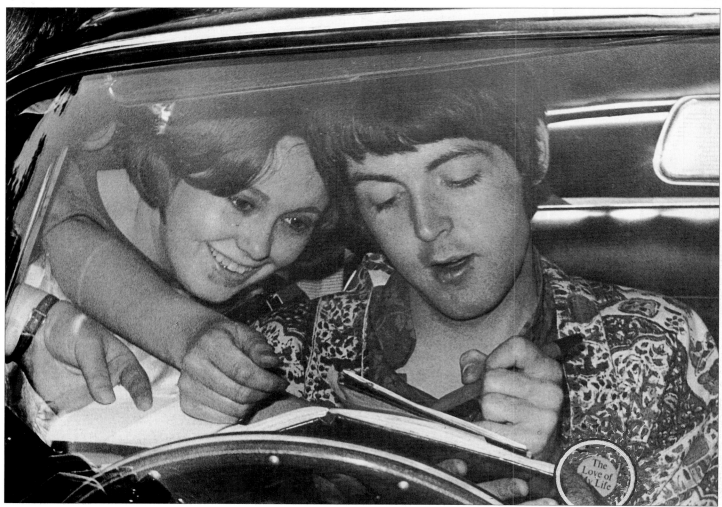

Holiday time

Ringo heads off to Athens for a break with the
Harrisons, wife Maureen remaining at home, heavily
pregnant with their second child. It was around this
time that The Beatles entered into serious negotiations
to buy a Greek island haven for themselves, where
they could escape the endless intrusions on their
privacy. The group pull out of the deal at the last
minute after Greek officials try to use it for publicity
and propaganda purposes.

Paul and John return home from Greece.
Opposite: Paul with Jane Asher and four-year-old Julian Lennon.

Proud Dad

Ringo, with camera at the ready, arrives at Queen Charlotte's Hospital to visit Maureen and new baby son Jason, who was born the previous day.

Opposite above: Ringo and mother-in-law, Mrs Florence Cox. As Zak was named by Ringo, a fan of Western films, Maureen claims her turn by naming the new arrival - after the Greek mythological hero.

The Beatles become interested in transcendental meditation after attending a lecture by the Maharishi Mahesh Yogi in London (*opposite above*).

The Maharishi is going on to hold a conference in Wales, and all The Beatles decide to attend. Ironically, what is intended as a spiritual retreat turns into a scrum involving media and fans as news of the trip leaks out.

Paul at Euston Station, preparing to leave for Bangor, North Wales, where the conference on transcendental meditation is being held.

Below: John's £1000 floral make-over of his Rolls-Royce causes quite a stir. The Phantom V had been black, oozing Establishment, sobriety and respectability. Six weeks at Fallon's coachworks company, Chertsey, puts a stop to all that.

Opposite: Paul at Newquay during the filming of *Magical Mystery Tour.*

Taking them away - the Magical Mystery Tour

Above: No mystery here: the bus is simply too wide for the narrow Devon bridge and becomes well and truly stuck. It is an inauspicious start for the *Magical Mystery Tour*, Paul's pet project, conceived back in April, for a film with no form or script. It is September before shooting starts, a matter of days after Brian Epstein's death.

Opposite: On location in the West Country. Widecombe Fair and Newquay are among the stop-off points on the *Magical Mystery Tour*.

Left and overleaf: Paul and George pictured at the memorial service to Brian Epstein, held on 17 October at the New London Synagogue, Abbey Road.

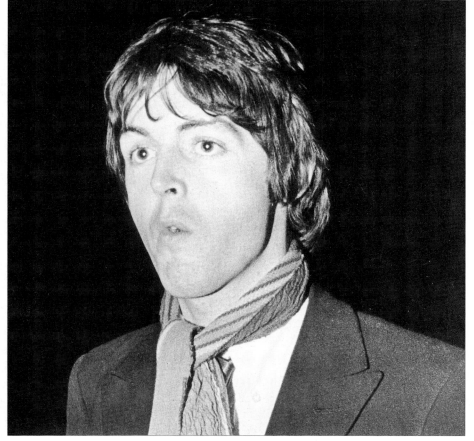

How I Won The War

The day after Epstein's memorial service, Paul, George and Ringo, with partners and friends, attend the première of *How I Won The War* at the London Pavilion.

Below: John and Cynthia join the other Beatles for a front row view.

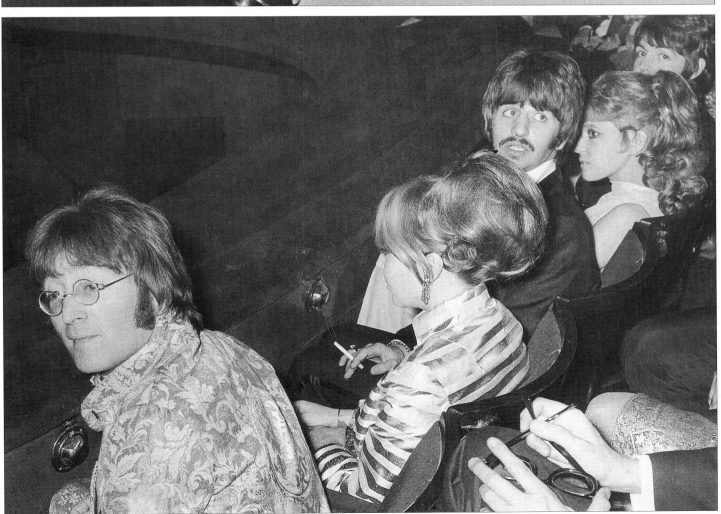

Ringo Sweet as Candy

Ringo looks to further his solo acting career by taking a minor part in the film *Candy*. Swedish beauty queen Ewa Aulin plays the nymphette of the title role.

Above: The director, Christian Marquand, shows Ringo how to look like a sex-mad Mexican gardener.

The Lennons and the Harrisons arriving at the Apple Boutique, Baker St, the first venture of their company which bears the same name.

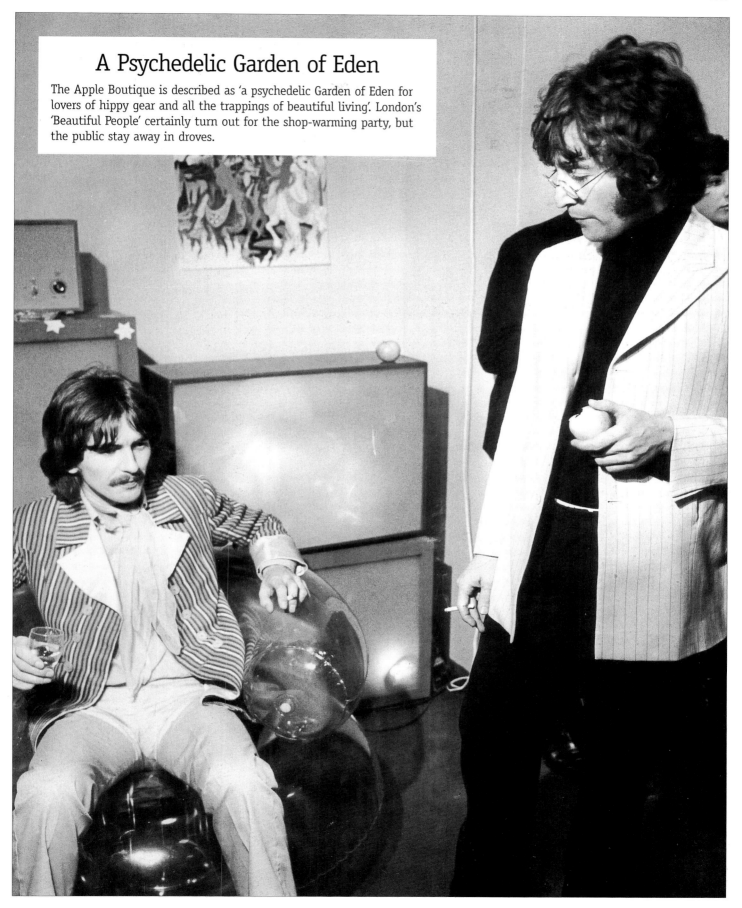

A Psychedelic Garden of Eden

The Apple Boutique is described as 'a psychedelic Garden of Eden for lovers of hippy gear and all the trappings of beautiful living'. London's 'Beautiful People' certainly turn out for the shop-warming party, but the public stay away in droves.

Magical Mystery...

Just before Christmas, The Beatles throw a party at the Royal Lancaster Hotel to launch the *Magical Mystery Tour* film. Guests are told to wear 'something magical' and all The Beatles themselves arrive in fancy dress.

The film is screened on Boxing Day, and is promptly panned by the critics. Although there are some moments of Beatle magic, much of the film comes across as a rather self-indulgent home movie and The Beatles' lack of skill and experience in production is only too evident.

Facing the music; Paul admits to mistakes, but does not regret making the film. The title should have informed people that there would be no plot or form, he says, adding: 'Was the film really so bad compared with the rest of the Christmas TV? Frankie and Bruce's (Messrs Howerd and Forsyth) show just wasn't funny, and you could hardly call the Queen's Speech a gasser.'

Chapter Six

1968

With A Little Help From My Friends

At the beginning of February, all four Beatles and their partners flew out to India to attend a three-month course in transcendental meditation at the Himalayan retreat of the Maharishi Mahesh Yogi. Ringo and Maureen had had enough after less than two weeks; the spicy vegetarian food did not agree with them and nor did the regime of chanting, meditation and mass praying. Paul and Jane stayed for only five weeks, but he claimed on his return that the trip had been a success and had done him good. The others left after nearly two months, when they heard rumours that the Maharishi had tried to enlighten some of the female members on the course in a physical rather than a spiritual way - although this later turned out to be just malicious gossip. George continued to pursue his interest in Indian culture and the Hindu religion, but the Maharishi was now out of the picture for good.

The Beatles turned their attention back to business, announcing the formation of Apple Corps Ltd. The plan was that Apple would have several divisions covering such areas as music, films, electronics, merchandise and the arts, and one of its functions was to provide creative people with funds to get them started – not in a philanthropic way, but as a business investment. It was a great idea in theory and Paul and John took it very seriously and went into the office regularly to direct operations. However, there was no one to organize everything on a proper business footing and to question if the funds going out would bring back any sort of return. The company soon became a source of easy money to every self-styled innovator, artist or hippy who happened to come through the door - and also to Apple executives and staff, who had lavish salaries, bought cars on their expense accounts and made the long lunch into an art form. It was to be some time before The Beatles realized what was happening and tried to take action.

Meanwhile a new Beatles film was ready for release: *Yellow Submarine*, a full-length animated feature film that had been two years in the making. It was based on one of The Beatles' earlier songs and they were consulted at the beginning, but they were not involved in working out the final concept or in developing the storyline. Even the voice-overs were spoken by actors, although the band did write a few new songs, as well as filming a short cameo appearance which was inserted near the end. The film did not do very good business in Britain because of poor distribution, but it went down very well in America and was highly regarded by the critics, often being referred to as 'the best film The Beatles never made'.

John attended the première accompanied by Yoko Ono. He had first met her two years previously and soon felt he had discovered a kindred spirit. In May of 1968 he invited Yoko to his home while Cynthia and Julian were away on holiday and from that moment they were inseparable; by the end of 1968 Cynthia and John were divorced. Another Beatles romance had also hit the rocks: although they had announced their engagement the previous Christmas, Paul and Jane Asher had split up for good by July – partly because of his growing friendship with American photographer Linda Eastman.

Throughout this period the group had been in the studio working on their double LP, *The Beatles* – which soon commonly became known as the *White Album* to distinguish it from the name of the band. One unexpected advantage of their long stay in India was that it had removed them from their usual surroundings and provided an ideal environment in which to develop their music. When they came back, both John and Paul had written quite a few songs and there were now

enough for the new album. Unfortunately it was not long before problems surfaced. The Beatles were now much less a group and more four individuals, each intent on doing his own thing. Paul and John did not really like each other's new songs, and George felt that his were being dismissed. On top of this, Yoko was soon ever-present in the studio, sitting next to John and whispering suggestions into his ear, encouraging him in his most extreme and avant-garde ideas. The other three bitterly resented her presence, as until then no outsiders had been allowed in the recording studio itself when they were working – even wives and girlfriends had only been welcome to watch from the control room. Meanwhile, Ringo was becoming increasingly unhappy with his role in the group. He could be ignored for hours at a time as the others worked out the words and harmonies of a song, and after criticism of his drumming one day, he walked out. He was soon persuaded to return, but deeper problems remained and this was the beginning of the end of The Beatles.

Below: Bring in the clown; George and John sample Apple's hospitality.
Previous page: John and Yoko with balloons, at the opening of his exhibition, 'You Are Here'.

1968: Chronology

25 January	John and George attend an Ossie Clark fashion show in London, at which Pattie is one of the models
6 February	Ringo appears live on Cilla Black's TV show, *Cilla*
15 February	John, Cynthia, George and Pattie fly to Rishikesh, India, to study Transcendental Meditation for three months under the Maharishi Mahesh Yogi
19 February	Paul, Jane, Ringo and Maureen fly out to join the others
1 March	Ringo and Maureen have had enough and return to Britain
15 March	The single 'Lady Madonna'/'The Inner Light' is released in the UK (18 March in the US)
26 March	Paul and Jane leave for England
12 April	John, Cynthia, George and Pattie arrive back in London
11 May	John and Paul fly to New York for five days, where they announce the setting-up of their Apple business venture
14 May	John publicly denounces the Maharishi on NBC-TV's *The Tonight Show*
17 May	The film *Wonderwall*, with music by George, has its world première at the Cannes Film Festival, but it does not prove to be a box office success
22 May	John and Yoko Ono appear in public together for the first time, attending a launch party and Press conference for another Apple Boutique
30 May	The Black Dyke Mills Band records Paul's composition 'Thingumybob' for a television series of the same name, which starts transmission on 2 August
7 June	Paul and Jane Asher attend Mike McCartney's wedding in North Wales
18 June	The National Theatre's production based on John's book, *In His Own Write*, opens at the Old Vic in London
21 June	Apple Corps buys new premises at 3 Savile Row
1 July	John's first art exhibition, *You Are Here*, opens in London
17 July	The Beatles' animated film, *Yellow Submarine*, has its world première at the London Pavilion

20 July	Jane Asher announces that her relationship with Paul is over
31 July	The Beatles' Apple Boutique on Baker Street closes down; they also relinquish control of their second clothing store in Kings Road
22 August	Cynthia sues John for divorce on the grounds of his adultery with Yoko Ono
23 August	Ringo quits The Beatles during recording sessions for the *White Album*
26 August	The single 'Hey Jude'/'Revolution' is released in the US (30 August in the UK)
3 September	Ringo rejoins The Beatles
8 September	A pre-recorded film clip promoting 'Hey Jude' is shown on *Frost On Sunday*
30 September	Hunter Davies' authorized biography, *The Beatles*, is first published in the UK
18 October	John and Yoko are charged with possession of cannabis and obstructing the police
1 November	The first solo project by a Beatle is released in the UK, *Wonderwall Music*, George's soundtrack for the film (2 December in the US)
8 November	John and Cynthia are divorced
8 November	George's songwriting contract with Northern Songs expires and is not renewed
11 November	John and Yoko's album, *Unfinished Music No 1 - Two Virgins*, is released in the US (29 November in the UK)
22 November	The LP *The Beatles* (better known as the *White Album*) is released in the UK (25 November in the US)
28 November	John pleads guilty to possessing cannabis to protect Yoko
18 December	John and Yoko appear together inside a white bag at the Royal Albert Hall

George returning from India. He had just completed
his first film score, composing and producing the
soundtrack for the film *Wonderwall*.

Opposite above: New four-piece band Grapefruit must
have hoped for even a fraction of the success of the
pop luminaries ranged behind them (*l to r:* Brian
Jones, Donovan, Ringo, John, Cilla Black, Paul). The
occasion was a Press reception at the Hanover Grand,
London, to mark the launch of the group's debut
single 'Dear Delilah'. The band, who had been
discovered by head of Apple Terry Doran, would make
little impact on the charts, however. 'Dear Delilah'
peaked at No 21, while their only other chart entry
was 'C'mon Marianne', which reached No 31.

Opposite below: John, Cynthia and George at the
Revolution Club, Mayfair, for a fashion show in which
Pattie takes to the catwalk. Next to John is Alexis
Mardas, otherwise known as Magic Alex, Apple's
electronics wizard.

We've got to hide ourselves away...

Above: Paul and fiancée Jane Asher head off with Ringo and Maureen to the Maharishi's private residence in India. The Lennons and Harrisons had left a few days earlier. They were looking forward to 'locking themselves away' from the world for a while, according to Paul.

Below and opposite: Paul and Jane arrive back in London after five weeks in India.

Meditation

Paul's verdict on the Maharishi? 'Great feller...down-to-earth...no flashy cars.' Paul says that he and Jane both plan to meditate for an hour each day: 'Meditation is great. I'd recommend it to anyone'. In reality, The Beatles would all eventually conclude that the Maharishi offered no signpost along the road to spiritual enlightenment.

The Big Apple

Where else could John and Paul announce the founding of the Apple Corps
but in New York? The philosophy behind the Apple organization was to
help others to help themselves; a lot of people soon take the idea literally -
helping themselves to Apple's resources.

Returning five days later, each brandishing the symbol of the newly-formed empire. A client list that includes James Taylor and Mary Hopkin - as well as The Beatles themselves - ensures that Apple Records is profitable from the beginning; other branches of the corporation soon degenerate into chaos and financial disaster.

Opposite: The Harrisons fly out to Nice. Although the destination is France, George's spiritual home is still India; his interest in the religion, culture and music of the country will endure.

Opposite below right and overleaf: Ringo and Maureen en route to Cannes. Ringo reveals that his diffidence about his own acting talent led him to reject several starring roles - including playing Dr Watson in a Sherlock Holmes film - choosing instead the minor part of the gardener in *Candy*.

In his Own Write

John and Yoko at the National Theatre for the first night of *In His Own Write*, a play adapted from two of Lennon's books and based loosely on his own childhood. With John and Yoko (*opposite below left*) is the play's co-producer, Victor Spinetti.

The Harrisons and Starrs returning from a trip to America, where George had taken part in the film *Raga*, with Ravi Shankar. In the same party is Cream guitarist Eric Clapton, one of George's best friends. When George and Pattie later drift apart, she will embark on an affair with Clapton and they subsequently marry. Clapton's song 'Layla' is believed to have been written with Pattie in mind.

Opposite and overleaf: Paul shows his musical eclecticism by turning his talents to the big brass sound. The occasion is the recording of a new McCartney composition, 'Thingumeybob', for the TV programme of the same name. It had originally been recorded in the studio, but Paul realized the sound wasn't quite right. Enter the Black Dyke Mills Band, Shipley, Yorkshire, for their moment of glory. Paul records both an indoor and outdoor version of the piece, and later says that the outdoor version will probably be used for the show, as it has a more authentic bandstand sound.

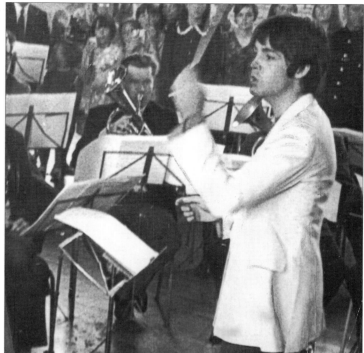

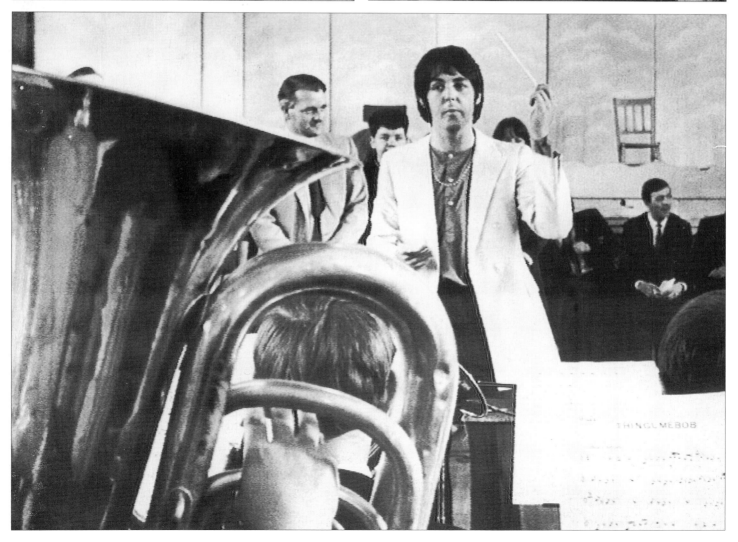

Back to his roots...

John goes back to his art college roots; he holds an exhibition at the Robert Fraser Gallery, Mayfair, consisting of a display of 50 charity boxes. The exhibition is entitled *You Are Here* and is dedicated to Japanese avant-garde artist Yoko Ono.

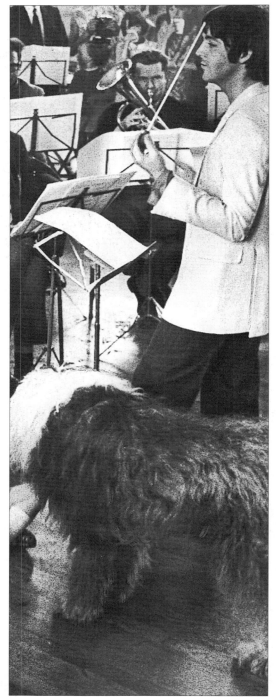

I Love You...

At the exhibition, John publicly declares his love for
34-year-old Yoko, who is still married to American film
director Anthony Cox.

And our friends are all aboard

It's like Beatlemania all over again as the group attend the London première of *Yellow Submarine*. Apart from the soundtrack, The Beatles' contribution to the film is minimal; they did not even select the song on which the animated feature would be based.

Opposite above left: Paul at his father's Wirral home, on the day after it is announced that his five-year-long relationship with Jane Asher is over.

Opposite: For once the hysteria is not generated by The Beatles in person. It is the closure of the Apple Boutique and the giving away of all the left-over stock that draws the massive crowds.

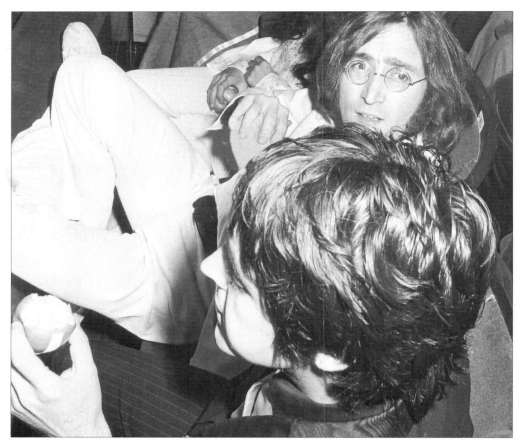

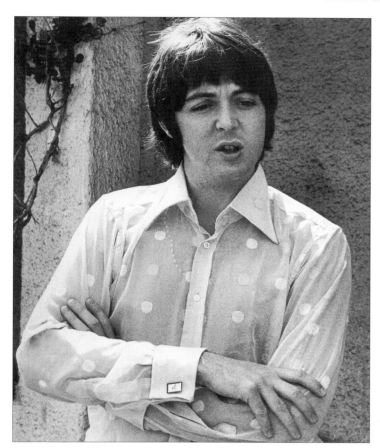

Hey Jude

Paul with Apple recording artist Mary Hopkin. Her song 'Those Were The Days' tops the charts for six weeks in the autumn of '68. The song which it knocks off the top spot is 'Hey Jude' - which had spent just two weeks at No 1.

Below: Gear change. Madame Tussaud's employee Juliet Simpkins checks the detail on the latest Beatle outfits. This is the Fab Four's fifth fashion update - at a total cost of £1000 - since they were first exhibited in 1964.

Opposite: John and Yoko have now become inseparable, with Yoko even attending recording sessions. Her influence is already placing a strain on the group. Ringo actually quits The Beatles for a short time during the making of the *White Album*, but this is hushed up and he is later persuaded to return.

No more drugs

In October John and Yoko are charged with possession of cannabis at Marylebone Court and remanded on bail until 28 November.

John claims his drug-taking days are over as he is fined £150 for possession of cannabis. The charges against Yoko are dropped.

Opposite: Five-year-old Julian Lennon gets to see a circus with a difference: a rehearsal of *The Rolling Stones' Rock And Roll Circus*, featuring a host of stars performing circus and variety acts. John himself is down to do a spot of juggling, but the show never reaches the screen.

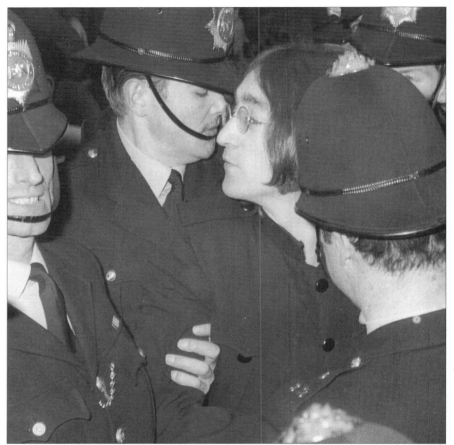

Chapter Seven

1969

All You Need Is Love

Their records were still outstandingly successful, but all four of The Beatles privately knew that as a group they were in trouble. Of them all, Paul was the most committed to keeping the band together and he also missed performing live in front of an audience. He reasoned that the main differences from the old days were that they no longer played together as a group and, because of spending weeks overlaying extra parts, took for ever to record each song. He decided that the solution lay in a return to performing live again and he tried to persuade the others to agree. Touring was definitely out, but they reluctantly decided to prepare for a concert or a television broadcast - with rehearsals being filmed for a documentary provisionally entitled *Get Back*, which was finally released as *Let It Be*.

The Beatles assembled at Twickenham Studios at the beginning of January, but almost immediately tensions within the group surfaced again, and this time it was George who walked out. He was persuaded to return, but the idea of doing a concert was shelved and they moved to their new Abbey Road recording studio to concentrate on making an LP. Keyboard player Billy Preston was invited to join them, which defused some of the tension and the recording proceeded. At the end of January, the group even played a live concert out of sight on the roof of the Apple building, which was filmed as part of the documentary. However, the finished tapes for the LP itself sounded so bad that The Beatles decided not to release it for the moment and went back to the studio to start again. Perhaps everyone knew it was the end, but this time they were all on their best behaviour and the result was *Abbey Road*, one of their finest LPs.

At the beginning of 1969, the group had also realized that they needed to do something about Apple Corps Ltd, which had been losing money hand over fist ever since it was formed. However, they disagreed on who should be put in control to set matters straight. John and Yoko wanted Allen Klein, a tough New York businessman who was already involved in the music business, and they convinced George and Ringo to join them in appointing his company, ABKCO, to sort out Apple. But Paul didn't trust Klein and wanted instead the New York firm of Eastman & Eastman – run by his girlfriend Linda's father and brother. The others felt the Eastmans would just be looking out for Paul's best interests, so although they were appointed as general counsel it was under Klein. The band had never done anything before that was not unanimously agreed, but this time Paul was outvoted.

As well as Apple, there were other major problems in their business affairs that came to a head in 1969. The Beatles lost their controlling interest in Brian Epstein's old company, NEMS, and in Northern Songs, the company which published their songs. This meant that they no longer owned the rights to any of their compositions, so valuable publishing royalties were now going to other people and other companies. Klein failed in his attempt to stop this happening, but he did manage to secure a vastly improved royalty deal from EMI for the group's American sales, which even impressed Paul.

Each of The Beatles was now developing an individual career. George had already released a solo album and was getting involved in projects with other artistes, while Ringo was developing his acting career by co-starring in *The Magic Christian*, a film with Peter Sellers, and also working on his first solo album. Paul had started on his album, *McCartney*, and he also got married at last, to Linda Eastman. John and Yoko had finally been able to marry and now began to give free rein to even their most outlandish ideas, including two 'bed-ins' for peace and appearing in public shrouded in large white bags. They also released avant-garde recordings by The Plastic Ono Band and produced films attempting to portray themselves spiritually rather than physically, all of which caused much adverse comment in the Press. John was now often absent when the others were recording Beatles numbers, but they just carried on without him.

Paul was still trying to keep the group together, but was fighting a losing battle. John had already told Allen Klein that he wanted to leave The Beatles, but had been persuaded not to say anything to anyone else since negotiations with EMI were at a delicate stage. However, when Paul started pushing again for them to do a series of live performances, John announced his intentions to the others as well. They all agreed to keep it quiet for the moment, so as far as the public were concerned everything was continuing as normal – whereas in fact Paul was now the only one who still wanted to be a Beatle.

Below: John and Yoko at a Press conference following a trip to Vienna.
Previous page: Alone at last; Paul and Linda off on honeymoon.

1969: Chronology

2 January	The Beatles begin filming *Get Back*, which is eventually retitled *Let It Be*
10 January	George walks out, but is persuaded to return
13 January	The LP *Yellow Submarine* is released in the US (17 January in the UK)
30 January	The Beatles give their last live performance on the roof of the Apple office building in central London
31 January	For their last filmed performance, The Beatles play 'The Long and Winding Road', 'Let It Be' and 'Two of Us'
3 February	Allen Klein becomes The Beatles' business manager
4 February	The New York firm of Eastman & Eastman is appointed as general counsel to Apple Corps
13 February	Paul and Linda attend the launch of Mary Hopkin's debut album, *Postcard*
20 February	Ringo attends the world première of *Candy* in London
1 March	Ringo begins filming *The Magic Christian* with Peter Sellers
4 March	Princess Margaret visits the set of *The Magic Christian* at Twickenham Studios
12 March	Paul marries Linda Louise Eastman at Marylebone Register Office in London
12 March	George and Pattie are busted for cannabis possession
20 March	John marries Yoko Ono at the British Consulate in Gibraltar
25 March	John and Yoko begin their seven-day 'bed-in' for peace at the Hilton in Amsterdam, Holland
11 April	The single 'Get Back'/'Don't Let Me Down' is released in the UK (5 May in the US)
22 April	John formally changes his middle name to Ono during a ceremony on the roof of the Apple building
8 May	Paul refuses to sign a contract appointing Allen Klein's company, ABKCO, as business manager of several of The Beatles' companies
9 May	The second John and Yoko LP *Unfinished Music No 2 – Life With The Lions* is released (26 May in the US)
9 May	George releases his second solo LP *Electronic Sound* in the UK (26 May in the US)
26 May	John and Yoko begin their second 'bed-in' for peace, at the Queen Elizabeth Hotel in Montreal, Canada
30 May	The single 'The Ballad Of John And Yoko'/'Old Brown Shoe' is released in the UK (4 June in the US)
1 June	The Plastic Ono Band, formed of John, Yoko and a selection of acquaintances, records 'Give Peace A Chance' during the 'bed-in'
1 July	Yoko and John, with her daughter Kyoko and his son Julian, are involved in a bad car crash while touring Scotland
8 August	All four Beatles are photographed walking along the zebra crossing outside EMI studios in North London, for the cover of *Abbey Road*
20 August	All four Beatles are together for the last time inside a recording studio, for a mix and album running order session at Abbey Road
22 August	The Beatles are photographed together for the last time, in the grounds of John and Yoko's home, Tittenhurst Park
28 August	A daughter, Mary, is born to Linda and Paul
28 August	George attends a Press conference in Sydenham for the Radha Krishna Temple
1 September	John, Yoko, George, Pattie, Ringo and Maureen see Bob Dylan in concert at the Isle of Wight Pop Festival
13 September	John decides to quit The Beatles, while on his way to Toronto, Canada, to perform a concert with The Plastic Ono Band
20 September	Allen Klein negotiates an increased royalty rate for The Beatles with Capitol/EMI
26 September	The LP *Abbey Road* is released in the UK (1 October in the US)
6 October	The Beatles single 'Something'/'Come Together' is released in the US (31 October in the UK)
20 October	The Plastic Ono Band release a single, 'Cold Turkey'/'Don't Worry Kyoko (Mummy's Only Looking For Her Hand in the Snow)', in the US (24 October in the UK)
20 October	John and Yoko release *Wedding Album* in the US (7 November in the UK)
25 November	John returns his MBE to the Queen
2 December	George joins the Delaney & Bonnie & Friends tour on stage during a concert in Bristol
10 December	John and Yoko meet the parents of James Hanratty, as they plan to make a film proving his innocence
11 December	The world première of *The Magic Christian* at the Odeon, Kensington, attended by Ringo, Maureen, John and Yoko
12 December	Another LP, *Live Peace in Toronto*, is released by The Plastic Ono Band worldwide
14 December	John and Yoko – or possibly two stand-ins - appear in a white bag in 'A Silent Protest' about the hanging of James Hanratty
15 December	The Plastic Ono Band, including John and George, plays a charity concert for UNICEF at the Lyceum Ballroom in London
30 December	John is featured in a three-part ITV programme, *Man of The Decade*, along with John F. Kennedy and Mao Tse Tung

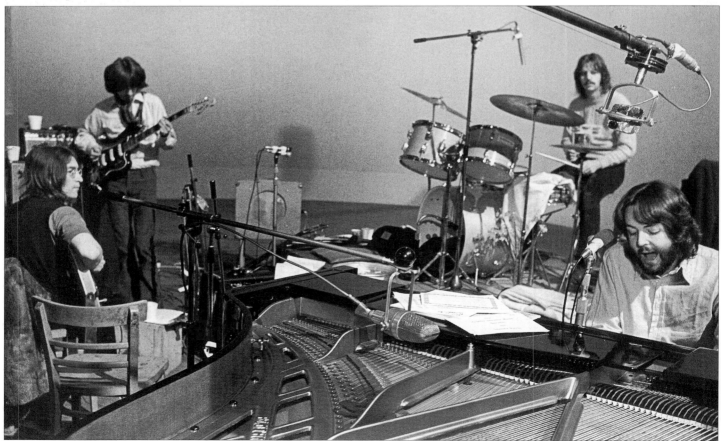

Let It Be

Filming the studio sessions for *Let It Be*.

Paul to marry?

Below: The rumour-mill is in overdrive concerning the last bachelor Beatle. Paul's name is linked with American photographer Linda Eastman, a 25-year-old divorcee with a six-year-old daughter.

Opposite: Linda Eastman takes flak from Paul's adoring female fans as the couple leave the Apple building in Paul's Mini. Paul has jettisoned the Castro-style beard which he sported for the celebrated Apple rooftop session a week earlier.

Right: The buck stops here. George declares an end to extravagant charitable giving. It follows a statement from John that they would all be broke in six months if the Apple Corporation continued haemorrhaging money at the present rate.

Paul and Linda at a launch party for Apple recording artist Mary Hopkin's debut album, held at the GPO Tower. The album had been produced by Paul (*opposite below*).

Opposite above: The couple attend the première of *Isadora* at the Odeon Theatre, St Martin's Lane.

It's official

On 11 March the rumours are proved to be true; Marylebone Register Office is booked for the following morning. Laid-back Paul buys the wedding ring which cost £12 'just before the shop shut'.

By Beatles' standards it is a quiet affair. There are no guests, and outside the register office photographers easily outnumber the assembled fans. Predictably, those who do turn up are mostly female and mostly distraught. Even so, Paul and Linda play safe and enter the building by a side door - past the dustbins (*above*).

At last...

Paul's best man is brother Mike McGear, of Scaffold fame, reversing their roles of the previous year, when Paul did the honours at Mike's wedding. Two hours after the register office ceremony, Paul and Linda have their marriage blessed by the Rev. Noel Perry-Gore, at St John's Wood Parish Church.

Surviving the crowds

Linda takes the opportunity to scotch Press reports that she is an heiress with family connections to Eastman-Kodak. 'I've been done, where's the money,' quips Paul.

George and Patti drugs charge

George and Patti are remanded on bail for cannabis possession at Esher and Walton Magistrates' Court (*below*), and are later fined £250 each on the drugs charge (*opposite*).

Right: Business as usual; the McCartneys have no immediate honeymoon plans and Paul gets straight back to work. He is seen here leaving Olympic Studios in London at 3.45 am after a recording session with Jackie Lomax on 13 March.

John and Yoko's turn to marry

Just eight days after Paul and Linda's wedding, John and Yoko Ono marry secretly in Gibraltar, then stage a very public 'bed-in' at the Amsterdam Hilton. 'Stay in bed, grow your hair' is the couple's anti-violence, anti-war message.

John and Yoko returning from Vienna on 1 April, where they saw the world première of *Rape*, their controversial production whose aim was to analyse the effect of blanket, intrusive TV coverage on an individual's life. In it, a girl is relentlessly pursued by a camera crew, who invade her life but refuse to speak to her. (*and overleaf*)

Mirror image

John and Yoko invariably mirror each other in their attire. Here they opt for all-white outfits as they leave for Geneva in April.

Opposite: Paul leaving the Apple offices, following yet another meeting regarding the troubled corporation's finances. The rift between the members of the group widens as Paul wants to bring in New York law firm Eastman and Eastman - Linda's father and brother. The others are suspicious and favour American businessman Allen Klein. Paul is outvoted, bitterly resenting the accusation of nepotism.

The Magic Christian

Ringo plays Peter Sellers' son in Terry Southern's satire *The Magic Christian*. The film's soundtrack features a McCartney song, 'Come And Get It', performed by Badfinger, a group signed to Apple.

Ringo and Peter Sellers throw their money around at a party celebrating the end of shooting. Each of the 300 guests invited to the Mayfair gaming club was given $1 million on arrival - but the faces on the notes bore an uncanny resemblance to Messrs Starr and Sellers and the money was valid only in the club casino.

The Ballad of John and Yoko

Five-year-old Kyoko Cox, Yoko's daughter by her previous marriage, flies in from New York on her own, to be met by her mother and famous new step-father. Meanwhile, Yoko makes her mark on the charts. The Beatles take 'The Ballad of John and Yoko' to No 1 in June; in the same month she and John record 'Give Peace A Chance', with a group of ad hoc musicians, The Plastic Ono Band. It reaches No 2.

Opposite left: Ringo makes sure his latest release gets into shot as he takes a break after the film is completed. Working on *The Magic Christian* had been a respite from the troubled Beatles' recording sessions, in which Ringo sometimes found himself sidelined, with Paul taking over on drums.

*Opposite righ*t: George returning from holiday in Sardinia. Like Ringo before him, George had actually quit The Beatles earlier in the year, following studio disagreements. Although he too returned a few days later, the cracks were now becoming impossible to paper over.

Kindred Spirits

George finds a group of kindred spirits at London's Radha Krishna Temple, a Hindu sect which trains people in the process of self-purification.

Opposite: Paul and Linda at the première of the film *Alfred The Great*.

Above: Yoko gets to grips with her new kitchen as she and John finally take up residence at Tittenhurst Park, a 60-acre estate with a mansion near Ascot. Cost: £145,000.

Hare Krishna

Members of Radha Krishna Temple shave their heads and ban drugs, alcohol and 'sex without children'. The 'Hare Krishna Mantra' becomes the unlikeliest pop hit of the year, peaking at No 12.

Opposite below: Just fans, like everybody else. John, George and Ringo, with spouses, are faces in a 150,000-strong crowd, all of whom have come to see Bob Dylan perform at the Isle of Wight pop festival in September.

From humble roots...

A far cry from 10 Admiral Grove where Ringo once lived in Liverpool, his new house in Kenwood (*opposite above*) has seven bedrooms, a heated swimming pool and nearly an acre of garden.

Opposite below: He also still owns a big house on the exclusive St George's Hill estate in Weybridge, which he bought in 1965, as well as a third home in Elstead.

James Hanratty

John and Yoko at a photo-call with James Hanratty's parents, and fellow-campaigner Edith Whicher.

The Lennons take up the case of James Hanratty, the man hanged in 1962 for the murder of Michael Gregsten in a lay-by on the A6 the previous year. John and Yoko announce that they plan to make a film of the infamous case, the anomalies in which played a part in the abolition of the death penalty.

Below: A seven-o'clock shadow of his former self. John's beard all but disappears for a while - by all accounts at Yoko's request.

Ringo, with Spike Milligan and Lulu, recording
a music and comedy show for Yorkshire TV to be
transmitted on Christmas Eve.

'War is over'

'... if you want it.' That's the Lennons' Christmas message to the world as they leave for Toronto on a peace crusade.

Chapter Eight

1970

Revolution

At the beginning of 1970, John and Yoko hit the headlines again. An exhibition of John's lithographs at the London Arts Gallery was raided by the police and eight erotic pictures depicting him and Yoko on their honeymoon were confiscated. John had also been taking heroin regularly and early in the year he entered a clinic to be cured of his addiction. Ringo's film, *The Magic Christian*, had its première in New York in February and although the film did not do well, his performance was complimented. He also released his LP, *Sentimental Journey*, which was not well received by the critics but did briefly enter the American charts. George was working on his new LP, *All Things Must Pass* and Paul was putting the finishing touches to his first album, *McCartney*.

All The Beatles' contractual affairs were in a mess, and Allen Klein discovered that, despite what they had been led to believe, *Yellow Submarine* did not constitute the third in their three-film contract with United Artists. However, there had been enough material filmed for *Get Back*, their proposed television documentary, to turn it into a full-length feature film instead – which they could sell to UA. There was also the LP recorded at the same time, which had not been released due to its poor quality. None of The Beatles wanted to have anything more to do with this, so Allen Klein appointed American producer Phil Spector to try and make something of it. His trademark was a dramatic, heavily orchestrated 'wall of sound' that had been used to great effect on other artistes' songs, but which was in total contrast to the way The Beatles normally recorded.

When the LP was ready for release, Paul was horrified to discover what had been done to it and in particular that his song 'The Long And Winding Road' had been almost swamped by the addition of a full orchestra and a female choir. He tried to insist that his original version was restored, but both Klein and the other Beatles ignored his protests. They also tried to delay the planned release of *McCartney*, so that it would not clash with the release of the Beatles LP and film, both now retitled *Let It Be* after one of Paul's songs. It was all too much, and in the press release that went out with advance copies of McCartney, Paul said that he had no plans to work with The Beatles again, and that he had not missed them while making his new LP. This was taken as an announcement that he was leaving The Beatles and the news prompted headlines in newspapers all round the world. The irony was that although Paul had been the first to say anything publicly, he was the last to make the decision that The Beatles were finished.

The film and LP *Let It Be* were released just afterwards, and the LP shot up the charts on a wave of nostalgia – even though most critics decided it was poor in quality and by no means showed The Beatles at their best. 'The Long And Winding Road' was also released as a single in America at the same time, and despite Paul's reservations went straight to No 1. *McCartney* was an international success, as was George's LP, *All Things Must Pass*. John's single, 'Instant Karma', had been a big hit earlier in the year and his LP, *John Lennon/The Plastic Ono Band*, went into the top twenty. Only Ringo was not doing so well, with his second LP, *Beaucoups of Blues*, getting a positive reception but only just making it into the charts. However, his best was yet to come.

Although The Beatles as a group were officially no more, with each member set on a solo career, the business side of things was by no means easy to resolve. The four of them were still legally tied together until 1977 by The Beatles & Co, the company they had formed three years earlier. Under the terms of their agreement, all the income that any of them made, even

from their solo albums, was to be split four ways. In addition, Paul remained seriously unhappy about Allen Klein's involvement in his affairs, even more so after he realized that Klein had pocketed around £5m in his first year of handling The Beatles. He had also been told by the Eastmans of the rumours about Klein in America, where quite a few lawsuits had been filed against him and where his unscrupulous business methods were well known. He couldn't just opt out of the agreement with the other Beatles so the only way out for him was to dissolve the partnership. At the end of December he filed a lawsuit in London seeking a dissolution of The Beatles & Co and the appointment of a receiver to sort out the band's affairs.

Below: George with Ravi Shankar at the start of an Indian Arts Season at the Royal Festival Hall.
Previous page: Ringo and Maureen arriving back from the US première of *The Magic Christian* in New York.

1970: Chronology

3-4 January	Three Beatles, without John, participate in their last recording session during John's lifetime, performing George's song 'I, Me, Mine' for the LP *Let It Be*
15 January	*Bag One*, an exhibition of lithographs by John, opens
16 January	John's exhibition is closed for obscenity and the police confiscate eight lithographs depicting him and Yoko
20 January	John and Yoko have their hair cropped in Denmark
6 February	A single, 'Instant Karma'/'Who Has Seen The Wind', is released by John and Yoko in the UK (20 February in the US)
26 February	An LP, *Hey Jude*, is released in the US
6 March	The Beatles' single 'Let It Be'/'You Know My Name (Look Up The Number)' is released in the UK (11 March in the US)
12 March	George and Pattie move into Friar Park, a mansion in Henley-on-Thames, Oxfordshire
27 March	Ringo releases his first LP *Sentimental Journey* in the UK (24 April 1970 in US)
10 April	Newspapers around the world carry Paul's statement that The Beatles will never work together again
17 April	Paul's first solo LP *McCartney* is released in Britain (20 April in the US)
23 April	John and Yoko go to Los Angeles to undertake a course of primal therapy with Dr Arthur Janov
27 April	The court declares that John's lithographs are not indecent and they are returned
8 May	The Beatles LP *Let It Be* is finally released in Britain (18 May in the US)
9 May	Ringo and Maureen fly to Nice to be guests of honour at the screening of *Woodstock* at the Cannes Film Festival

11 May	A Beatles single 'The Long and Winding Road'/'For You Blue' is released in the US
13 May	The Beatles' film, *Let It Be*, receives its world première in New York. None of the group attends
7 July	George's mother, Louise, dies
20 September	George attends the opening night of 'A Festival of Arts of India' at the Royal Festival Hall, London
25 September	Ringo releases his second LP, *Beaucoups of Blues*, in the UK. (28 September in the US)
15 October	Release in the US only of Ringo's single 'Beaucoups of Blues'/'Coochy-Couchy'
11 November	A daughter, Lee Parkin, is born to Ringo and Maureen Starkey
23 November	George releases a single, 'My Sweet Lord'/'Isn't it a Pity' in the US. (In the UK the B side is 'What Is Life' and the single is released 15 January 1971)
27 November	George releases his third solo LP *All Things Must Pass* in the US (30 November in the UK)
8 December	John does a major interview with *Rolling Stone*, which is published in two parts on 21 January and 4 February. It is later also published as a book, *Lennon Remembers*
11 December	John releases another album, *John Lennon/The Plastic Ono Band* worldwide
31 December	Paul files a lawsuit in the London High Court to dissolve the partnership, The Beatles & Co, and appoint a receiver to handle the group's affairs

Going solo

The mood within The Beatles is now firmly on individual projects; After *The Magic Christian* Ringo turns his attention to a solo album, *Sentimental Journey*. Even Paul has finally accepted that the break-up of The Beatles is irrevocable.

Below: Paul had begun recording tracks for his own solo album, *McCartney*, at the end of '69. This creates even more friction, as Allen Klein and the other members of the group try to prevent its release clashing with *Let It Be*.

All Things Must Pass

George renews his friendship with Ravi Shankar (*overleaf*) during an Indian Arts Season, held at the Royal Festival Hall in September. On the musical front, George enlists Phil Spector to produce his first solo project, the ambitious triple album *All Thing Must Pass*. They spend six months in the studio - compared to the six days Ringo spent making *Beaucoups of Blues*. It is well received by critics, and the record-breaking cover price does not deter the fans.

Opposite: Paul and Linda, looking serenely happy as The Beatles' split reverberates round the world.

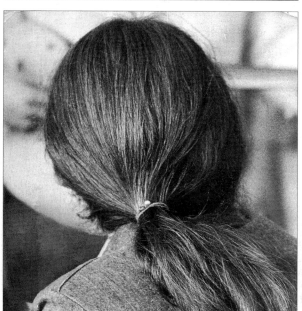

Opposite: John and Yoko pictured in November, just prior to the release of the album *John Lennon/The Plastic Ono Band,* which reaches No 11 in the charts. It was around this time that Paul wrote to John on the subject of the dissolution of Apple. John replied with a postcard which read: 'Get well soon. Get the other signatures and I'll think about it.' It was responses such as these which precipitated Paul's decision to sue.

Below: George with Ravi Shankar.

Chapter Nine

1971

You Never Give Me Your Money

The High Court case to dissolve The Beatles' company was heard in London during February and March and Paul was the only Beatle to attend, supported by his wife, Linda. The others still believed that Allen Klein was their saviour so they felt that Paul was merely out to cause trouble. At the time he was also disliked by many fans and was having a hard time in the Press because they all blamed him for breaking up the group. He claimed he was not going through the court case just for himself, but for all the Beatles, since their entire empire was about to vanish into someone else's pocket. His counsel pointed out that Paul would actually be better off sticking to the terms of the original agreement, since the most successful record of that financial year had been George's single, 'My Sweet Lord', which had become the best-selling single of 1971. However, it soon became apparent that Allen Klein had taken at least $500,000 more than he was entitled to on The Beatles' American royalty deal, and the High Court judge finally ruled in favour of Paul. The other three Beatles were furious, but at the same time felt a sense of release - now they were really free to pursue individual careers.

George was initially riding high, with both his last LP and his latest single at the top of the charts. Unfortunately an American music publisher then claimed that 'My Sweet Lord' plagiarized a hit of the 1960s, 'He's So Fine', by the Chiffons.

The court battles were to go on for years, before George was defeated and had to pay out thousands of dollars. Meanwhile his interest in India led him to organize *Concert For Bangladesh*, two concerts at Madison Square Garden in New York in aid of famine victims. The first was of Indian music specially composed by Ravi Shankar and the second boasted an all-star line-up, all performing for free, including George, Ringo, Bob Dylan and Eric Clapton. The concerts, with an accompanying album and film, raised an enormous amount, well over $10m. Unfortunately a great deal of money was creamed off by the various record companies involved and by the tax authorities – even though all the proceeds were for charity – and only a small percentage of the total actually made it to Bangladesh.

John released one of his most critically acclaimed solo albums, *Imagine*, which topped the charts in both Britain and America. The songs were much more gentle - more commercial and less avant-garde - than those John had released previously, but also included a bitter attack on Paul in a song called 'How Do You Sleep?'. This was also the year that John was allowed back to America. For several years he had been refused entry because of his drug convictions, but in September 1971 the authorities relented and John and Yoko flew to New York for a short visit, which turned into a permanent stay. The Press in Britain had done nothing but ridicule them and their beliefs and make fun of Yoko as an artist, but in America they were much less critical and seemed more open to new ideas.

Ringo surprised everybody. Since his first two LPs had not been that well received, many people were beginning to think that he would not succeed in a solo career. However, he now released his new single, 'It Don't Come Easy', recorded with George and their old friend from Hamburg, Klaus Voormann, and it quickly reached No 5 on both sides of the Atlantic. He soon proved this wasn't just a flash in the pan either, as he followed it up with three more hit singles and an LP in the following couple of years.

Paul's second solo album, *Ram*, also found critical success, although his catchy songs were much more popular with the fans than with the music Press. Unlike the others, whose albums were all done with new bands, both of Paul's LPs featured only himself, with the odd contribution from Linda.

He still missed performing live and he was keen to get out on the road again, so in August he formed his own new band, Wings. The line-up included several accomplished musicians – and also Linda on keyboards even though she was a photographer with little musical skill. The music world was highly critical of her abilities, making fun of her voice and deriding her for appearing to muscle in on Paul's group. It was not the first time Linda had suffered bad Press - general coverage of her had often been critical after their marriage, for very little apparent reason.

But the burning question on everyone's mind seemed to be: would The Beatles ever get back together again? It was the subject of endless speculation in the Press, and each individual Beatle could be sure that he would be asked the question at least once in every Press conference.

Below: Paul's father, Jim, and stepmother, Mary, join in the celebrations at the launch of Wings.
Previous page: John and Yoko on their way to Majorca.

1971: Chronology

19 February	The hearing for the dissolution of The Beatles & Co partnership commences in the London High Court
19 February	Paul releases his first single, 'Another Day'/'Oh Woman, Oh Why' in the UK (22 February in the US)
23 February	George is fined and banned from driving for a year
26 February	Paul appears in court to give evidence in the Beatles case. The others choose not appear in person, but they do send written affidavits
12 March	John and Yoko release a single, 'Power To The People'/'Open Your Box' in the UK. In the US the B side is 'Touch Me' and the single is released on 22 March
12 March	The High Court judge rules in favour of Paul
9 April	Ringo's single, 'It Don't Come Easy'/'Early 1970', is released in the UK (16 April in the US)
15 April	*Let it Be* wins an Oscar for Best Original Song Score
12 May	Paul and his family and Ringo and Maureen go to Mick Jagger's marriage to Bianca
15 May	The world première of two of John and Yoko's films, *Apotheosis (Balloon)* and *Fly*, at the Cannes Film Festival
17 May	Paul's second solo LP, *Ram*, is released in the US (28 May in the UK)
1 August	*A Concert For Bangladesh* is staged by George at Madison Square Garden in New York
28 July	George releases a single, 'Bangla Desh'/'Deep Blue', in the US (30 July in the UK), proceeds of which go to famine relief and the homeless in Bangladesh
2 August	Release in the US only of Paul's single, 'Uncle Albert'/'Admiral Halsey b/w Too Many People'
3 August	Paul announces the formation of his new band, Wings
13 August	Paul's single, 'Back Seat Of My Car'/'Heart Of The Country', is released in the UK only
3 September	John and Yoko fly to New York for a short visit, which turns into a permanent stay
13 September	A second daughter, Stella Nina, is born to Paul and Linda
8 October	John's LP, *Imagine*, is released in the UK (9 November 1971 in the US)
8 November	Paul holds a fancy dress party at the Empire Ballroom, London, to launch Wings
10 November	The world première of *200 Motels*, in which Ringo appears in a cameo role, is held in New York
15 November	The world première of *Blindman*, in which Ringo appears in a cameo role, is held in Rome
23 November	The world première of *Raga*, in which George appears in a cameo role, is held in New York
1 December	John and Yoko release the single, 'Happy Christmas (War Is Over)'/'Listen, The Snow Is Falling' in the US (24 November 1972 in the UK)
4 December	John publicly attacks Paul in the letters page of *Melody Maker*
7 December	Paul's new band Wings release their first LP, *Wild Life* in the UK (22 May 1980 in the US)

The long and grinding road

Opposite: Paul and Linda pictured during the nine-day hearing at the High Court.

Below: Ringo takes a break from the acrimonious legal proceedings as he flies out to Zurich.

Right: Paul and Linda with 18-month-old Mary.

Linda to join the band...

Paul reveals that they are soon to depart for France, where he will record a new album featuring just himself and Linda. It is one of the earliest indications that Linda will play a part in Paul's future musical output.

Ringo and Maureen at a farewell party for Peter Sellers, who is about to become a tax exile in Ireland. Tax liability is also one of the central issues in The Beatles' legal wrangle.

Opposite: Paul's second solo album, *Ram*, is about to hit the shops as the Lennons pay a visit to Majorca. Over the summer, John takes to his Tittenhurst Park Studios to record *Imagine*. The personal spat between John and Paul is continued in both the visual and lyrical content of these two albums.

Jagger's Wedding

The McCartneys en route to Mick Jagger and Bianca Perez-Mora's wedding in St Tropez.

Below left: The Starrs are also invited to the Jaggers' wedding, which brings Ringo and Paul a little too close for comfort.

It Don't Come Easy

Ringo's 'It Don't Come Easy' was riding high in the charts at the time of the trip to Mick Jagger's wedding.

Opposite: John at Apple, soon after the release of his single, 'Working Class Hero'.

It's easy if you try...

With the release of *Imagine* still several weeks away, Yoko takes centre stage with the publication of her book *Grapefruit*. Yoko had published 500 copies of her collection of 'instructional poems' some seven years earlier, and had sent John a copy. The content was a series of enigmatic thoughts, such as: 'Draw a map to get lost' and 'Smoke everything you can, including your pubic hair.'

Opposite: Paul and Linda host a gala evening at the Empire Ballroom, Leicester Square, to launch their new group, Wings.

Fledgling group

Drummer Denny Siewell (*left*) and Denny Laine, the ex-Moody Blues
guitarist/vocalist complete the Wings line-up.

Chapter Ten

After The Beatles

The Long and Winding Road

For the first few years of the Seventies there was still substantial bad feeling between Paul and the other three former Beatles. Their business affairs took a while to untangle, as Allen Klein and ABKCO did not reach the end of their term as business managers of Apple and the other Beatles companies until the end of March 1973 and The Beatles & Co partnership was not formally dissolved in the London High Court until January 1975.

Meanwhile, Paul went back to touring with Wings and their music steadily improved. Unfortunately two members of the band quit in August 1973, just before they were due to fly to Lagos, Nigeria to record their next album. Paul, Linda and the remaining member, Denny Laine, carried on without them and produced their best album to date, *Band On The Run*. In the next few years Wings had a constantly changing line-up, but their follow-up album, *Venus And Mars*, was equally successful. The world tour made in 1975/76 was a sell-out, and Paul later said he made more money in this period than he ever had with The Beatles.

John and Yoko's friends in New York included a whole crowd of left-wing radicals and political activists and the American government soon took note and began moves to get him deported. John fought the action, but the strain had its effect on his marriage and towards the end of 1973 he left Yoko in New York and went to Los Angeles with their secretary, May Pang. What was supposed to be a temporary separation turned into a fifteen-month 'lost weekend', as John settled into a house with Keith Moon and Ringo and the three of them over-indulged in drink and drugs.

Despite this, John managed to produce two good albums, *Walls and Bridges* and *Rock 'n' Roll*, but he still pined for Yoko and finally pulled himself together and returned to her in New York in January 1975. After their son, Sean, was born later in 1975, John announced that he was taking five years off to play with his baby while Yoko carried on working. They settled in New York permanently, since the deportation order against John had finally been lifted and he was granted his Green Card.

Ringo followed up the success of 'It Don't Come Easy' with three more hit singles and an LP, *Ringo*, in 1973 on which John, Paul and George were all featured – although Paul at no point recorded at the same time as John or George. Still, it was the nearest thing to a Beatles reunion so far achieved. His acting career also continued, including what many believe was his best film, *That'll Be The Day*, with David Essex. After this high point, Ringo's musical career began to go downhill. His marriage also hit the rocks, which was when he joined John and Keith Moon on their bender in Los Angeles. He and Maureen divorced acrimoniously in 1975 and after this Ringo spent much of the remainder of the Seventies wandering round the world, being seen with various foreign girls in various countries and drinking too much.

After having said he would never tour again, George did one tour across America in 1974, which was not a great success; although the concerts were a sell-out, a throat infection had made his voice hoarse. Fans were also angry that he refused to play many Beatles numbers and said his new music was too experimental. He came close to a nervous breakdown afterwards – things were not going well in his musical career and his marriage to Pattie was breaking up. George and Pattie divorced in 1977, and in 1978 George married Olivia Arias, whom he had met when she came to work as a secretary at his record company. The wedding had been postponed because of the death of George's father, and was rescheduled after the birth of their first and only child, a boy called Dhani. Towards the end of the Seventies, George became involved in the British film industry when he helped the Monty Python team raise funding for their film, *The Life Of Brian*. Afterwards he formed his own production company, HandMade Films, which made quite a few successful films, mainly based on British subjects and locations.

At the end of the Seventies, Paul's doubts about Allen Klein were proved to have been prophetic, when Klein was jailed in America after it was found that there were major irregularities in his accounting for the income he had creamed off George's *Concert for Bangla Desh* project. By this time, relations between Paul and the others were much improved. Paul had played with John while visiting Los Angeles in 1973, and Paul, George and Ringo had reunited for a jam session at the garden party after Eric Clapton's wedding to the former Pattie Harrison in May 1979.

Having completed his promised five years looking after Sean, John returned to recording and brought out a new album, *Double Fantasy*, just in time for his son's fifth birthday in 1980. The reviews were good and John seemed happy and full of enthusiasm in interviews he gave around this time. On 8 December, as he came out of the Dakota building where he lived in New York, he was stopped by Mark Chapman and signed a copy of *Double Fantasy* for him. Chapman then waited outside the building all day until John returned from the studio much later that night. He fired five shots at point-blank range and although John was rushed to hospital he was pronounced dead when he arrived.

The sense of grief and outrage at his death was overwhelming all around the world, but was even more hysterical in America. In Britain there had been little news of him over the previous few years and he was regarded as someone who had become a bit eccentric and retired from the cutting edge of music. In America he had captured the hearts of those opposed to the war in Vietnam and his song 'Give Peace A Chance' had become their anthem. Many of them felt they had lost an inspirational leader. On 14 December Yoko called for ten minutes of silence to be observed at 7.00pm GMT around the world in his memory and throughout December the airwaves were full of the sound of 'Imagine', one of his best-loved songs.

Ringo had recovered from his alcoholism and had met a new partner, American actress Barbara Bach, while filming *Caveman* early in 1980. They were involved in a serious car crash in London the same year, but both escaped without injury. He was badly shaken by John's death and the following year he left America and with Barbara returned to Britain, where they were married in April. After his return he also patched things up with Maureen and became closer to his children, much of whose growing-up he had missed while roaming round the world. His musical career faltered for a while, but he still did some acting and in 1984 he recorded the narration for a series of *Thomas the Tank Engine*, for many children becoming for ever the cheeky voice of Thomas.

Even before John's death, the Eighties began badly for Paul. He had twice been refused permission to tour Japan with Wings because of his previous drug convictions, but finally the Japanese authorities had relented. Arriving in Japan at the beginning of January, Paul was searched by customs men at Narita Airport and they found a large stash of cannabis. He was thrown into prison and the local British Consul warned that they might try to make an example of him with a sentence of several years. Luckily after only eight days he was released and deported back to England. It was the final straw for the remaining members of Wings, and although they continued to record for several further months they had split up for good by the end of the year. Paul went on to release a series of solo albums, but unfortunately also decided to get involved in making another film. He wrote both the songs and the script for *Give My Regards To Broad Street*, which was savagely attacked by the critics and died at the box office.

After John's death, George became even more obsessive about his privacy. Throughout the Eighties he was perhaps best known for his involvement in HandMade Films, although he never used his Beatle persona to promote the pictures they made or attended star-studded premières. He also released a best-selling solo album, *Cloud Nine*, and toured with Roy Orbison, Tom Petty, Jeff Lynne and Bob Dylan as The Travelling Wilburys. Gardening became one of his overwhelming interests, and he spent a great deal of time and energy growing exotic plants in his 36-acre garden in Oxfordshire.

One unexpected result of John's death was that the other three Beatles started collaborating again. Ringo had always got on well with both Paul and George - and with John before his death - but George and Paul now tried to bury their differences. George's tribute to John, 'All Those Years Ago', which was released not long after his death, featured backing by Paul and Ringo. Right back in the Seventies The Beatles had planned to produce a documentary that would tell their story in their own words, tentatively titled *The Long And Winding Road*. The project had suffered the same fate as many others after their break-up - the four of them could never agree on what and how things should be done. Now everyone else who had ever been connected with The Beatles seemed to be bringing out retrospectives and anniversary tributes, and the three remaining Beatles agreed it was perhaps time to have their final say.

The original idea was that this documentary would be a straightforward record telling the true story, since they all felt that everyone else had got it wrong. They started by going back to the archives to see what was there, and were surprised by the amount of material that turned up - forgotten interviews, alternative recordings, unfinished songs and comic out-takes. Some of the material had already found its way on to bootleg records, but much had just been gathering dust at Abbey or in EMI's storerooms around the world. Gradually the project turned into more than just the story of the group and became a collection of pretty much everything The Beatles had ever done, right back to when they were schoolboys. It ended up being both a television documentary and three double LP/CDs, all entitled *The Beatles Anthology*.

Below: Ringo and George on stage during the Prince's Trust Rock Concert in June '87.
Previous page: Three Beatles and a wedding: Ringo and Barbara get married.

Much of the material could never have been released at the time it was recorded because it was either unfinished, early versions of songs, or spoiled/rejected takes, but such material was now interesting because it showed how things had developed - and was invaluable to fans and to music historians. Paul, George and Ringo were interviewed specially for the documentary, as were three of The Beatles' intimates: George Martin, their recording engineer, Neil Aspinall, their roadie and general assistant, and press officer Derek Taylor. John was included in the form of old interviews, mainly from his solo days. The most controversial part of the project, however, was the inclusion of two brand-new Beatles songs, which were also released as singles.

For years people had been asking if The Beatles were going to get back together again, and even John's death did not stop them - they just substituted Julian Lennon in the line-up. The answer had always been no, but when Paul, George and Ringo were collecting material, Yoko had sent them some tapes of John's that included several unfinished songs. This sparked the idea that the remaining Beatles could finish them off, adding further instrumentation and harmony vocals. The approach they took mentally was that John had started the song, but was now going off somewhere and had left them to finish it - which was not so different to how they had sometimes worked in the old days. Many people said it couldn't be done and that the three of them were very ill-advised even to try, but they were determined to prove the doubters wrong.

Towards the end of 1995, amidst the sort of hype and publicity that was reminiscent of The Beatles' heyday in the Sixties, the first single, 'Free As A Bird', and the first double LP/CD were released, in conjunction with the television documentary. Newspapers ran whole pages devoted to the 'Fab Four' and magazines around the world brought out special editions. The three Beatles themselves did not do much to publicize the project - it was enough that they had set the ball rolling. Even after 25 years The Beatles were still major news - and the new singles did sound like proper Beatles songs, with both going into the top ten in the charts.

During the remainder of the Nineties, Ringo continued to drum for other artistes and toured America and Europe again with his own bands. These have been made up of a variety of featured players - including his son, Zak, who is also an accomplished drummer. George kept out of the limelight and tended his garden, but was still involved in the music business and was by no means forgotten - when he was stabbed by an intruder in his house at the end of 1999, he received messages of sympathy from all over the world. Paul continued to record and make live appearances, tried classical music and animated films, and was deeply involved in environmental issues. He received a knighthood in 1997, but not long afterwards his wife Linda died from cancer and he retreated into his private life for a time. He surfaced again to support his daughter, Stella, in her career as a fashion designer and since then has been moving back into the public eye once again. At the end of 1999, when the new Cavern Club in Liverpool was opened, he was the only former Beatle who turned up to play.

Although Paul, George and Ringo may perhaps record together in the future, they can never again be The Beatles without John. But in a way it doesn't matter, because Beatles music is still loved and played around the world, their records are being re-released on CD and no one can ever take away the effect they had on popular music. The group still exists in people's hearts and minds: The Beatles are for ever.

Below: Paul during Wings' '89/90 world tour.
Opposite: The full McCartney family arrives at Heathrow; (*from l to r*) Stella, James with Paul, Mary, Linda and Linda's daughter Heather.

Back off Boogaloo

Right: Ringo's solo career continues in great style, with the release of his second hit single, 'Back off Boogaloo'. He also directs the filming of T. Rex in concert at the Empire Pool Wembley for *Born to Boogie*, made by Apple Films. Ringo himself appears in the film, in a jam session shot at a recording studio.

Opposite: Maureen, Ringo, Pattie and George off to the Cannes Film Festival to see the movie of George's *Concert for Bangla Desh*.

Below right and overleaf: After spending the first few months of 1972 playing unannounced at universities around Britain, Paul and his band Wings begin their first proper tour with concerts in France, Germany, Switzerland, Denmark, Finland, Sweden, Norway and The Netherlands. Despite the sniping in the Press, Linda is still an essential part of the line-up.

That'll Be The Day

Ringo looked great in *That'll Be the Day* (*below right*), which was set in the late 1950s. It was almost a recreation of his youth, since his character was based in a summer holiday camp similar to the Butlin's camps he had worked in with Rory Storm and the Hurricanes before he joined The Beatles.

After filming had finished Ringo began work on his new LP, *Ringo*, but although things were going well professionally, personally he and Maureen were on the verge of splitting up.

Opposite above left: Paul and Linda during Wings' UK tour.

Opposite below left: 'That's my daddy' - Stella joins Paul and Linda at a photo-call.

Opposite above right: Even in the Seventies, Paul and Linda were involved in charitable causes. In November 1973 they made a surprise visit to the Toy For a Sick Child Fund in Piccadilly, where two-year-old Stella donated her teddy, Fruity.

Opposite below right: John in Los Angeles, during his separation from Yoko.

On your bike...

Now that all the legal problems of The Beatles break-up were far behind him, Paul seemed more relaxed. He developed a reputation as a family man, spending his free time with Linda and the children.

Below: The McCartneys on the move again, this time off to New Orleans where Paul was recording for his new LP, *Venus and Mars*. Paul had recently met up with John and George in New York, so the Press was full of rumours about The Beatles reforming.

Wings over water...

Below right: Paul chats to George Harrison during a party for Wings, which was held by Capitol Records aboard the liner *Queen Mary* at Long Beach.

Right: George was going through a bad time during this period. His marriage to Pattie had hit the rocks, and his last LP, *Dark Horse*, had quickly been dubbed 'Dark Hoarse' by the critics because of the poor state of his voice.

Below and opposite below: Another tour for Wings, this time their first, and only, tour round the world. The first section began with concerts all round Britain, after which they moved on to Australia.

Opposite above: Linda relaxes during the tour, while Paul entertains Stella and her playmate, Tamsy Lee.

Wings at Wembley

Opposite: Wings give two concerts at the Empire Pool, Wembley, playing to 8,000 people. Two 'journalists' from the USSR also attended one of the concerts, and Paul announces that he hopes to tour Russia in the near future.

After his split from Maureen, Ringo was seen around the world with several different women, including Nancy Andrews and Shelley Duvall. At one point he even became engaged to Nancy, but it was short-lived.

Out on the town...

Right: Paul attends the première of *Billy*.

Below right: At the wedding reception for Mike Leander, Gary Glitter's manager, and Penelope Carter at the Ritz Hotel, Piccadilly.

Opposite above: Susan George and Marc Bolan join Paul and Linda at a backstage party at Olympia to celebrate Rod Stewart's comeback concert in 1976. Rod himself missed the party – he went home early to shake off a heavy cold.

Opposite below: Although they were expecting to have another girl, Paul and Linda's first son, James Louis, made his appearance on 12 September 1977. Linda took the first picture of him herself using a timing device, and was photographed doing so by the *Daily Mail*'s Press Photographer of the Year, Monty Fresco.

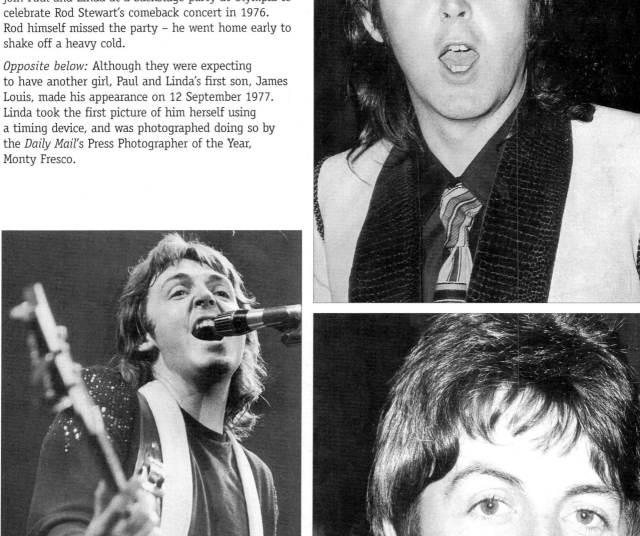

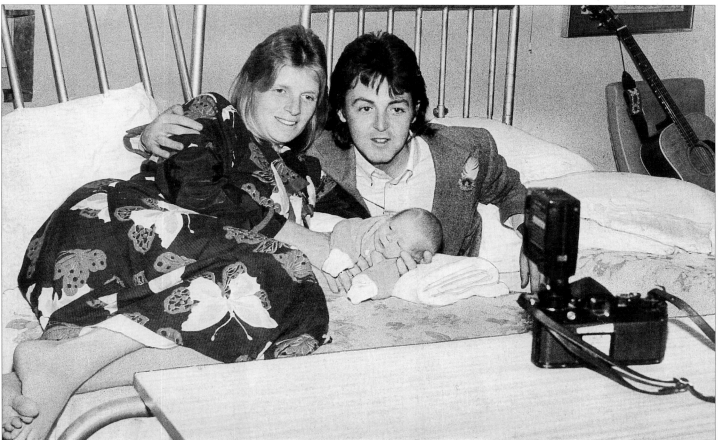

Things were finally looking up for George. He had a new love, Olivia Arias, a new hobby, Grand Prix racing, and a new hairdo, curly. His last LP, *33 1/3*, had been a critical success and his divorce from Pattie was finally sorted out, leaving him free to move forward.

Above and opposite: To promote their new LP, *London Town*, Wings took the Press on a boat ride down the Thames, with fish and chips to eat. Wings now consisted of Paul, Linda and Denny Laine, with two session musicians on guitar and drums to make up numbers.

Below left: George leaves the nursing home in Windsor, after Olivia has given birth to their first and only child, a boy who is called Dhani.

Opposite left: Ringo's last few records had not been successful, but he faces the Press in July 1978 to promote his new single, 'Tonight'. It was one of the few public appearances he made towards the end of the Seventies – with no film roles to speak of and his records flopping, he withdrew into his private life and refused to give interviews. His health problems also come to a head in April 1979 when he is rushed into hospital in Monte Carlo, close to death. His illness was part of the long-term after-effects of the peritonitis he suffered when he was six, which had led to him going into a coma for ten weeks and then spending over a year in hospital. This time, after a successful operation to remove five feet of intestine, Ringo is back on his feet by the end of the month.

George's problem (*below right*) is a little simpler – he ran over his foot with a tractor that he was using in the grounds of his home at Henley, near Oxford.

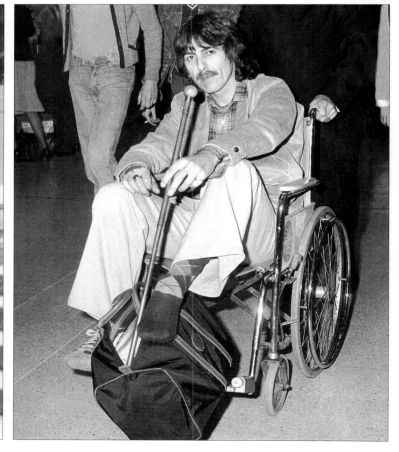

100 million albums later...

Paul is awarded the first rhodium disc by Norris McWhirter, editor of *The Guinness Book of Records*, for being the most honoured man in music. By their reckoning he has written 43 songs which have sold more than a million copies, has 60 gold discs and his sales of 100 million albums and 100 million singles make him the world's most successful recording artiste. The award sparks massive debate among musicologists, who claim it should really have gone to one of the classical musicians like Beethoven or Strauss.

Actress Victoria Principal is one of the stars who gather at the ceremony, held at Les Ambassadeurs Club in London.

Opposite below: Linda and Paul, with Denny Laine and his wife, relax at a party after Wings have played for charity at the Odeon, Hammersmith, along with Paul's collection of 'Rochestra' musicians. Their spot was at the end of a week-long season of concerts by top groups in aid of Kampuchean refugees and UNICEF.

Paul and Linda arrive at the Royal Court Theatre, Liverpool, where the evening before they played a free concert for the staff and pupils of Paul's old school, the Liverpool Institute, as well as a group of handicapped children. Wings continue to play at the Royal Court for a further three nights, as they start their UK tour.

Opposite and below: Where Paul goes, a selection of other McCartneys is sure to follow...

Eight days in jail...

Paul faces the Press at the gates of his Sussex farm, fresh from eight days in prison and deportation from Japan after a large stash of cannabis was found in his luggage. But things soon begin to look up when he receives two more music industry awards: Paul with Linda (*opposite below left*) arriving at the Café Royal to receive the Outstanding Music Personality at the British Rock and Pop Music Awards; later in the year, Yul Brynner (*opposite below right*) presents Paul with a Special Ivor Novello Award for his services to British music, at a West End celebrity lunch.

Opposite above left: Paul, still popular with all ages, is mobbed by fans wanting his autograph.

Opposite above right: Although becoming obsessive about his privacy, George is busy launching his company, HandMade Films, which involves travelling between London and the film capital of the world, Los Angeles.

Ringo and Barbara wed

After the trauma of John's murder, the remaining three Beatles and their families are glad to be gathering for a happy event: Ringo's wedding to Barbara Bach in London.

Below: George and Olivia run a gauntlet of Press photographers as they leave the Register Office after Ringo's wedding.

Opposite: As part of the celebrations for the seventh annual Buddy Holly Week, Paul and Linda attend a Rock 'n' Roll Dance Championship on 7 September at the Lyceum Ballroom in London. They both appear in costume, with Paul as a convincing Holly.

Holidays and trips...

After having been arrested and fined $200 each for possession of cannabis while on holiday in Barbados, Paul and Linda arrive back at Heathrow, where Linda is arrested again when a minute quantity of cannabis is found in her luggage.

Later, at Uxbridge Magistrates Court (*below right*), Linda claims that she thought the Barbadian police had removed all the drugs and that she was not aware she still had some in her possession. However, she pleads guilty to avoid a messy trial and was fined £75.

Opposite: Although Ringo may have been the poorest Beatle in the Eighties, with only around £20 million to his name, he and Barbara seem determined to have a good time. After a holiday in Tahiti in October 1982 (*opposite right*) they go on to Australia. They were soon leaving for another holiday in Montego Bay (*opposite centre left*), as well as going out on the town in London (*opposite bottom left*).

Give my regards to... Liverpool

Beatlemania makes a return to Liverpool, when Paul goes back to attend the British première of *Give My Regards to Broad Street* at the Odeon Cinema, and to collect a gold-framed scroll honouring him as a Freeman of the City. All of the Beatles had been made Freemen the previous year, but Paul is the first to come in person to receive the honour. Linda receives a silver salver in the same ceremony, held in Lime Street's Picton Library.

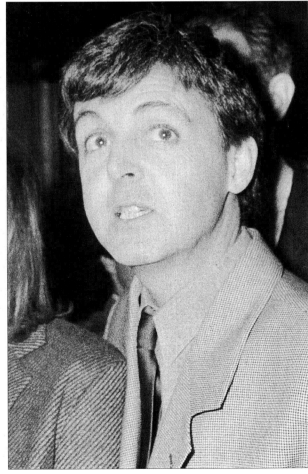

A celebration party at the Hippodrome night-club (*below right and opposite above left*), before the London première of *Give My Regards to Broad Street* at the Odeon, Leicester Square, is attended by Paul, Linda, Ringo and Barbara and Olivia Harrison. George can't make the première, because he is in New Zealand attending a literary luncheon to help Derek Taylor – once Brian Epstein's assistant and then The Beatles' Press Officer during their Beatlemania days - promote his new book, *Fifty Years Adrift*.

Opposite below: Ringo, always ready for a party, dresses in gold brocade for a Chelsea Arts Club masked ball with a Venetian carnival theme. Barbara wears an equally extravagant costume with a head-dress of gold roses.

Opposite above right: Ringo becomes the first grandfather Beatle when his daughter-in-law, Sarah Starkey, gives birth to a girl, Tatia Jane.

Camera shy

Paul is always ready to mess about for the camera. Here he is at his Soho office.

George Harrison's company, HandMade Films, picks up a fine collection of honours at The London *Standard* Film Awards in 1986. *My Beautiful Laundrette* takes top place as Best British Picture of the Year, while *A Private Function* receives the award for Best Screen Play as well as the Peter Sellers Comedy Award for Michael Palin's performance.

Meanwhile, filming of HandMade's latest venture, *Shanghai Surprise* starring Madonna, is not going so well. George spends some time on the set (*opposite*), both because of the problems and because a documentary about the making of the film is being shot for UK television's Channel Four.

In the frame

As well as supporting Paul in all his public ventures, such as the annual Buddy Holly Week (*right and opposite left*), Linda begins to develop her own career again throughout the Eighties.

Below: Linda with Paul and Billy Connolly at the launch party in 1982 of her book, *Linda's Pictures: A Collection of Photographs*.

Opposite right: After successful exhibitions of her photographs in London and Paris, Linda is invited to take part in a joint exhibition of 24 photographers, mounted by the Council for the Protection of Rural England. Each photographer is asked to take pictures of threatened sites around the country, and Linda chooses Fairlight, near Hastings, which is endangered by oil exploration.

Right: Some of Britain's top rock stars, including George and Ringo, gather to play a concert in honour of rock 'n' roll singer Carl Perkins.

Below: George also appears in Heartbeat '86, a concert at Birmingham's National Exhibition Centre to raise money for a local children's hospital, along with The Electric Light Orchestra and The Moody Blues.

Opposite above: Yoko began her first world tour with a private moment in the Amsterdam Hilton. Sitting alone in the centre of the bed in which she and John staged their first 'bed-in' for peace in Amsterdam exactly seventeen years ago, she talks to the Press about her life since his death. During the concerts, Yoko performs some of John's best-loved songs, including 'Imagine', and 'Give Peace a Chance'.

Opposite below: Although *Give My Regards to Broad Street* had been a box office disaster, *Rupert and the Frog Song* - its supporting film also made by Paul - was great entertainment. It went on to be honoured as the 1985 Best Selling Video at the British Video Awards.

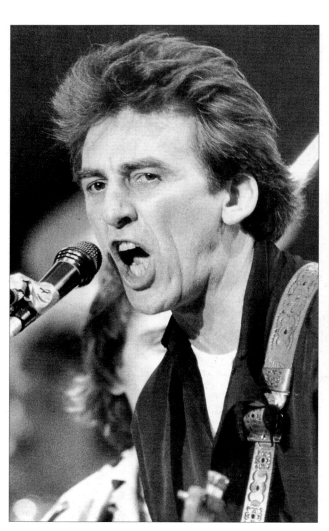

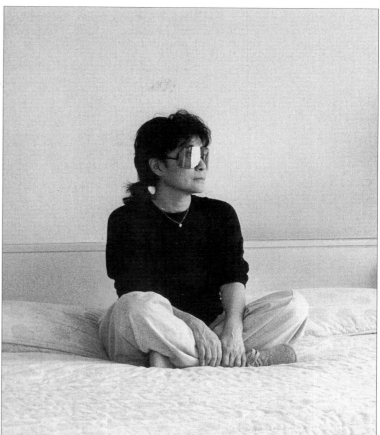

It was 20 years ago today...

Opposite: At a massive party to celebrate the 20th anniversary of the official release date of *Sgt Pepper's Lonely Hearts Club Band*, Paul cuts a slice of cake, helped by Linda and artist Peter Blake, who created the cover picture.

Back on stage again for the Prince's Trust Rock Concert in June '87, George's guests include Ringo, Eric Clapton, Elton John and Phil Collins.

Paul McCartney
...and The Crickets

Paul and Linda were by now both well-known for their efforts for charity, but perhaps even she was taken aback when Paul successfully bid £32,000 for a guitar signed by David Bowie and the Everly Brothers. The auction was in aid of the Nordoff-Robbins Music Therapy Centre for handicapped children, and at the end of the evening Paul agreed to sign the guitar himself and give it back to the charity to auction again the following year.

Opposite: Paul had always been a great fan of Buddy Holly, and after buying the rights to his songs in 1976 he had organized a Buddy Holly Week every year in September, to commemorate Holly's birthday. After a competition to write a new song in the style of Holly, Paul produced the winning entry, 'T-shirt' by Jim Imray, as a single for The Crickets, Holly's backing group. As well as using his Sussex studio to record the song, Paul himself also played keyboards on the backing.

Opposite above right: Chrissie Hynde, who was celebrating her own birthday, joins Paul at the party.

On the road again

Paul still loved performing in public, and at the end of the Eighties he formed a new band to back him during a twelve-month world tour beginning in July 1989. The line-up included Linda as usual, with guitarists Hamish Stuart and Robbie McIntosh, drummer Chris Whitten and keyboard player Wix. On tour Paul is the star, with the others merely a backing band. Refusing any sponsorship, Paul dedicated the tour to Friends of the Earth - which didn't mean that they received any profits but did give them a platform for their views in the programme.

Opposite below right: Paul finishes the Eighties with yet another award, a miniature gold copy of his own guitar, presented by the Performing Right Society for his contribution to pop music. At the lunch held at Claridge's Paul is given a standing ovation by guests, who included violinist Nigel Kennedy, Bee Gees Maurice and Robin Gibb, Bruce Welch from The Shadows, Chris Rea and song-writer Tim Rice.

Paul's world tour continues in January 1990 with concerts in Birmingham and London before he and his entourage return to America for another three months. In London Paul appears at Wembley Arena, opening the concert with a stunning show of lasers and film images covering the history of the world over the past 25 years.

Opposite below: While in the US, Paul meets up with Michael Jackson again. There had been rumours that they had fallen out after Jackson bought the rights to all the Lennon-McCartney songs for $47.5 million, but Paul assures everyone that they are still good friends.

Profits from the concert held in Liverpool during Paul's world tour were to be split between seven charities, but the overheads were so enormous that it only just broke even. Paul donated £100,000 of his own money instead.

Below: In 1991, having been a vegetarian for twenty years along with Paul and the rest of the family, Linda works with a major frozen food company in the UK to launch her own range of frozen pre-cooked vegetarian meals.

Simply the best

When *Q* magazine published its 100 Greatest
Stars of the Twentieth Century, based on
readers' votes, John Lennon was No 1, Paul
was next at No 2, Ringo came in at No 26
and George at No 36.

1972-99: Chronology

1972

8 Jan The triple LP of George's Bangladesh benefit concert, *The Concert For Bangla Desh*, is released in the UK (20 February in the US)

9 Feb Wings start an impromptu tour of British universities by appearing unannounced at Nottingham University

25 Feb Paul releases another single, 'Give Ireland Back To The Irish'/'Give Ireland Back To The Irish (version)' in the UK (28 February in the US)

28 Feb George and Pattie are injured in a minor car accident in Maidenhead

17 Mar Ringo releases his second single 'Back Off Boogaloo'/'Blindman' in the UK (20 March in the US)

18 Mar At the Empire Pool, Wembley, Ringo directs the filming of T. Rex in concert for the Apple film, *Born to Boogie*

May The film of *The Concert For Bangladesh* is shown at the Cannes Film Festival, after its world première in New York on 23 March

12 May Wings release their first single, 'Mary Had A Little Lamb'/'Little Woman Love' in the UK (29 May in the US)

21 May BBC Radio One begins a serial, *The Beatles Story*

5 Jun George and Ravi Shankar are given an award by UNICEF in recognition of their efforts in aid of refugees in Bangladesh

12 Jun John and Yoko release their double LP, *Some Time In New York City* in the US (15 September in the UK)

9 Jul Wings begin a European tour with a concert at Châteauvallon in France

10 Aug Paul and Linda are charged with possessing drugs in Sweden

30 Aug John and Yoko stage two charity concerts at Madison Square Garden in New York in aid of handicapped children

20 Sept Scottish police raid the McCartneys' farm and find cannabis plants

16 Oct Shooting of Ringo's new film, *That'll Be the Day*, begins in the UK

1 Dec Paul releases another single, 'Hi Hi Hi'/'C Moon' in the UK (4 December in the US)

14 Dec Ringo attends the world première of *Born to Boogie* in London

23 Dec The world première of John and Yoko's film, *Imagine*, on US television

1973

9 Mar Paul is fined £100 for growing five cannabis plants

18 Mar Wings play a benefit for Release at London's Hard Rock Café

23 Mar The first single from Paul and Wings, 'My Love'/'The Mess' is released in the UK (9 April in the US)

31 Mar Allen Klein and ABKCO reach the end of their term as business managers of Apple and other Beatles companies

2 Apr A pair of double LPs are released in the UK, *The Beatles 1962-1966* and *The Beatles 1967-1970* (19 April in the US)

12 Apr The world première of *That'll Be the Day* at the ABC cinema in Shaftesbury Avenue is attended by Ringo, Maureen, Paul and Linda

16 Apr Paul's TV film, *James Paul McCartney*, is shown on US television (10 May in the UK)

30 Ap Paul and Wings release an LP, *Red Rose Speedway*, in the US (4 May in the UK)

11 May Wings begin their first proper tour of the UK with a concert in Bristol

26 May George releases a single, 'Give Me Love (Give Me Peace On Earth)'/'Miss O'Dell', in the UK (7 May in the US)

30 May George releases another LP, *Living In The Material World* in the US (22 June in the UK)

1 Jun Paul releases a single of the James Bond theme that he has written, 'Live And Let Die'/'I Lie Around'

4 Jul Wings start another short tour of the UK with a concert in Sheffield

5 Jul The world première of *Live and Let Die* at the Odeon, Leicester Square, attended by all of Wings

24 Sept Ringo releases his single, 'Photograph'/'Down And Out' in the US (19 October in the UK)

Oct John separates from Yoko and flies to Los Angeles with their secretary, May Pang

26 Oct Paul releases 'Helen Wheels'/'Country Dreamer' in the UK (12 November in the US)

2 Nov John, George and Ringo sue Allen Klein for misrepresentation in the High Court, and Klein counter-sues

2 Nov John releases the LP, *Mind Games* and the single, 'Mind Games'/'Meat City' in the US (16 November 1973 in the UK)

2 Nov Ringo releases his LP, *Ringo*, in the US (23 November in the UK)

3 Dec Another single from Ringo, 'You're Sixteen'/'Devil Woman' is released in the US (8 February 1974 in the UK)

5 Dec Paul and Wings release *Band On The Run* in the US (7 December in the UK)

1974

15 Feb - Release in the UK of the Paul and Wings single, 'Jet'/'Let Me Roll It', from *Band On The Run* (18 February in the US)

18 Feb Ringo releases his single, 'Oh My My'/'Step Lightly' in the US. In the UK the B side is 'No No Song' and the single is released 9 January 1976

8 Apr Release in the US only of the Paul and Wings single 'Band on the Run'/'Nineteen Hundred and Eighty Five'

28 Jun Release in the UK only of the Paul and Wings single, 'Band On The Run'/'Zoo Gang', from *Band On The Run*

23 Sept John releases his single, 'Whatever Gets You Through The Night'/'Beef Jerky', in the US (4 October in the UK)

26 Sept John releases his LP, *Walls And Bridges* in the US (4 October in the UK)

18 Oct UK release of 'Walking in the Park with Eloise'/'Bridge Over the River Suite', by the Country Hams, a pseudonym for Paul and Wings with Floyd Cramer and Chet Atkins (2 December in the US)

25 Oct Paul releases his single, 'Junior's Farm'/'Sally G' in the UK (4 November in the US)

28 Oct Allen Klein loses his court case against John, George and Ringo

2 Nov George begins his solo tour of the US with a concert at the Pacific Coliseum, Vancouver

11 Nov Ringo releases his single, 'Only You'/'Call Me' in the US (15 November in the UK)

15 Nov Ringo releases his LP, *Goodnight Vienna* in the UK (18 November in the US)

16 Nov John has his first solo No 1 in the US, when 'Whatever Gets You Through The Night' reaches the top of the *Billboard* chart

18 Nov George releases his single, 'Dark Horse'/'I Don't Care Anymore' in the US only. In the UK the B side is 'Hari's on Tour (Express)' and the single is released on 28 February 1975

6 Dec George releases his single, 'Ding Dong'/'I Don't Care Anymore' in the UK only

9 Dec George releases his LP, *Dark Horse* in the US (20 December in the UK)

16 Dec First US release of John's single, '#9 Dream'/'What You Got' (31 January 1975 in the UK)

1975

Jan John returns to Yoko in New York

9 Jan The Beatles & Co partnership is formally dissolved in the London High Court

16 Jan Wings begin to record for their next album, *Venus and Mars*

27 Jan Release in the US only of Ringo's single 'No No Song'/'Snookeroo'

7 Feb Paul and Wings' single, 'Junior's Farm'/'Sally G' is re-issued in the UK only, with the A and B sides swopped round

17 Feb John releases his LP, *Rock 'n' Roll* in the US (21 February in the UK)

21 Feb Release in the UK only of Ringo's single 'Snookeroo'/'Oo Wee'

1 Mar John and Yoko appear together again in public, at the Grammy Awards in the US, where John is a guest presenter

3 Mar Linda is arrested and charged in the US with possession of cannabis

6 Mar	John issues a statement that his separation from Yoko is over
10 Mar	John releases a single, 'Stand By Me'/ 'Move Over Ms L' in the US (18 April in the UK)
24 Mar	Capitol Records in the US holds a party for Wings on the liner *Queen Mary*, which is docked at Long Beach
26 Mar	Ringo attends the London première of the film *Tommy* with his new girlfriend, Nancy Andrews
16 May	UK release of Paul and Wings' single, 'Listen to What the Man Said'/'Love in Song' (23 May in the US)
30 May	UK release of the Paul and Wings album, *Venus and Mars*
17 Jul	Ringo and Maureen Starkey are divorced
5 Sept	Release in the UK of Wings' single, 'Letting Go'/'You Gave Me the Answer' (29 September in the US)
9 Sept	Wings begin a world tour with a concert at the Gaumont cinema in Southampton
3 Oct	George releases his LP, *Extra Texture (Read All About it)* in the UK (22 December in the US)
7 Oct	The New York State Senate votes to reverse the deportation order against John, which he has been fighting for some years
9 Oct	A son, Sean Taro Ono, is born to John and Yoko
10 Oct	The world première in New York of *Lisztomania*, which includes a cameo appearance by Ringo
24 Oct	First release in the UK only of John's single, 'Imagine'/'Working Class Hero'
1 Nov	Wings continue their world tour, with a concert in Perth
21 Nov	Linda's US drug charge is dismissed
25 Nov	Ringo releases his LP *Blast From Your Past* in the US (12 December in the UK)
28 Nov	First UK release of the Paul and Wings single 'Venus and Mars'/'Rock Show'
8 Dec	George releases his single, 'This Guitar (Can't keep from Crying)'/'Maya Love' in the US (6 February 1976 in the UK)

1976

25 Jan	Ringo appears with Bob Dylan in a benefit concert for Rubin 'Hurricane' Carter in Houston
26 Jan	The Beatles' recording contract with EMI expires. Paul stays with EMI, but George and Ringo move to other labels. John does not sign with anyone
5 Mar	EMI releases a boxed set of all the original UK Beatles singles, as well as re-releasing them all individually, with one new issue, 'Yesterday'
20 Mar	Paul and Wings continue their world tour with several concerts in Europe, starting in Copenhagen, Denmark
26 Mar	Paul and Wings release their LP, *Wings at the Speed of Sound* in the UK only
1 Apr	Paul and Wings release their single, 'Silly Love Songs'/ 'Cook of the House' in the US (30 April in the UK)
3 May	Paul and Wings begin touring the US and Canada, with a concert at Fort Worth
23 Jun	Paul and Wings complete their world tour with three nights at the Forum, Los Angeles. Ringo joins them on stage during the final song of their encore and gives Paul a bunch of flowers

28 Jun	Paul and Wings release their single, 'Let 'em In'/ 'Beware My Love' in the US (23 July in the UK)
27 Jul	John finally gets his Green Card
7 Sept	George is found guilty of plagiarizing 'He's So Fine' for his hit song, 'My Sweet Lord'
7 Sept	After buying the rights to Buddy Holly's songs, Paul stages the first Buddy Holly Week in London, which becomes an annual event
17 Sept	Ringo releases his LP, *Ringo's Rotogravure* (27 September in the US)
19 Sept	Paul and Wings begin a short tour of Europe with a concert in Vienna
20 Sept	Ringo releases his single, 'A Dose of Rock and Roll'/'Cryin'' in the US (15 October in the UK)
15 Nov	George releases his single, 'This Song'/'Learning How to Love You' in the US (19 November in the UK)
19 Nov	George releases his LP, *33⅓* worldwide
22 Nov	Ringo releases his single 'Hey Baby'/'Lady Gaye' in the US (29 November in the UK)
10 Dec	Paul and Wings release their triple LP, *Wings Over America* in the UK

1977

10 Jan	All outstanding litigation between Allen Klein and The Beatles is settled
4 Feb	Wings release their single 'Maybe I'm Amazed' in the UK, a live version of Paul's original solo version
11 Feb	George releases his single, 'True Love'/'Pure Smokey' in the UK
4 Apr	The Beatles go to the High Court to stop the release of an LP recorded live in Hamburg in 1962; the judge decrees it can be released
29 Apr	First release in the UK of the LP *Thrillington*, by Percy 'Thrills' Thrillington, pseudonym of Paul McCartney (17 May in the US)
4 May	The live LP, *The Beatles at the Hollywood Bowl*, is released in the US (6 May in the UK)
25 May	*The Beatles Live! At the Star-Club in Hamburg, Germany, 1962* is released in the UK (13 June in the US)
31 May	Linda and Wings release a single, 'Seaside Woman', in the US under the pseudonym Suzy and the Red Stripes. It is released in the UK on 10 August 1979
9 Jun	George and Pattie are divorced
12 Septr	A son, James Louis, is born to Paul and Linda
16 Sept	Ringo releases his single, 'Drowning in a Sea of Love'/'Just a Dream' in the UK (18 October in the US)
26 Sept	US release of Ringo's LP, *Ringo the 4th* (30 September in UK)
11 Nov	Paul and Wings release their single, 'Mull of Kintyre'/'Girl's School' in the UK

1978

14 Jan	The first of LWT's *The South Bank Show* features Paul, with an interview and exclusive footage
22 Mar	Paul and Wings hold a Press conference during a Thames boat trip to promote their new LP, *London Town*

20 Mar	Paul and Wings release their single, 'With a Little Luck'/'Backwards Traveller – Cuff Link' in the US (24 March in the UK)
31 Mar	Official UK release of the Paul and Wings' LP, *London Town*
21 Apr	Ringo releases his LP, *Bad Boy* in the US (16 June in the UK)
26 Apr	Ringo appears in his own TV special, *Ringo*, on US television, with George making a cameo appearance. It is not shown in the UK until 2 January 1983
12 Jun	Paul and Wings release their single, 'I've Had Enough'/'Deliver Your Children' in the US (16 June in the UK)
21 Jul	Ringo releases his single, 'Tonight'/'Old Time Relovin'' in the UK
1 Aug	A son, Dhani, is born to George and his girlfriend, Olivia Arias
11 Aug	First UK release of Wings' single 'London Town'/'I'm Carrying' (21 August in the US)
2 Sept	George & Olivia marry

1979

14 Feb	George releases his single, 'Blow Away'/'Soft Hearted Hana' in the US. In the UK the B side is 'Soft Touch' and the single is released two days later on 16 February
14 Feb	US release of George's LP, *George Harrison* (16 February in the UK)
16 Feb	George releases his single, 'Blow Away'/'Soft Touch' in the UK. In the US the A side is 'Love Comes To Everyone' and the single is released on 11 May
15 Mar	Wings release their single, 'Goodnight Tonight'/'Daytime Night-time Suffering' in the US (23 March in the UK)
Apr	Ringo nearly dies from severe intestinal problems but has an operation in Monte Carlo
27 Apr	Allen Klein is found guilty of tax evasion in New York and is sent to prison
19 May	Paul, George and Ringo reunite for a jam session at a garden party celebrating the marriage of Eric Clapton to the former Pattie Harrison
8 Jun	UK release of Paul and Wings' LP, *Back to the Egg*, which is followed by a big party on the 11 June at EMI's Abbey Road studios
13 Jul	George releases his single 'Faster'/'Your Love Is Forever' in the UK
10 Aug	Paul and Wings release their single, 'Getting Closer'/'Baby's Request' in the UK
22 Aug	George publishes an autographed, limited edition book, *I Me Mine*. All 2,000 copies sell out quickly, despite the price of £148
24 Oct	The Guinness Book of Records presents Paul with a rhodium disc
16 Nov	Paul releases a single, 'Wonderful Christmastime'/ 'Rudolf the Red-Nosed Reggae' in the UK (20 November in the US)
24 Nov	Wings begin a UK tour with the first of three concerts in Liverpool
28 Nov	All Ringo's Beatles mementoes are destroyed when his house in the Hollywood Hills is burnt down

7&10 Dec	Wings play two nights at the Empire Pool, Wembley as part of their UK tour
29 Dec	Wings play in a concert for Kampuchean refugees and UNICEF at the Odeon, Hammersmith. Paul also gathers together a massive collection of musicians to form his 'Rockestra' to play three numbers

1980

16 Jan	Arriving in Japan to begin a tour, Paul is arrested for carrying cannabis
18 Feb	Ringo begins shooting *Caveman* in Mexico
26 Feb	Paul receives the Outstanding Music Personality award at the British Rock and Pop Music Awards at the Café Royal
27 Feb	Paul's 'Rockestra Theme' wins a Grammy award
11 Apr	Paul releases his single, 'Coming Up'/'Coming Up (live) - Lunch Box-Odd Sox' in the UK (15 April in the US)
9 May	Yul Brynner presents Paul with a Special Ivor Novello Award for his services to British music
16 May	UK release of Paul's LP, *McCartney II* (21 May in the US)
19 May	Ringo and his new girlfriend Barbara Bach are involved in a serious car crash in London, but escape without injury
13 Jun	Paul releases his single, 'Waterfalls'/'Check My Machine' in the UK (22 July in the US)
1 Aug	George forms his own film company, HandMade Films (Productions) Ltd
9 Sept	John and Yoko start an interview session for *Playboy* magazine, which lasts nearly 19 days
15 Sept	UK release of Paul's single, 'Temporary Secretary'/'Secret Friend'
22 Sept	Yoko signs a record deal for herself and John with Geffen Records
29 Sept	The first interview with John and Yoko for several years is published in *Newsweek*
24 Oct	First UK release of John's single, '(Just Like) Starting Over'/'Kiss Kiss Kiss' (27 October in the US)
17 Nov	John and Yoko release their new LP, *Double Fantasy* in the US and UK
26 Nov	The world première of *Rockshow*, a film of Wings' 1976 tour of the US, is held in New York
5 Dec	John tapes an interview for the magazine *Rolling Stone*
6 Dec	John and Yoko together record an interview for BBC Radio One
8 Dec	John and Yoko together record an interview for RKO Radio
8 Dec	John is shot dead at the age of 40 by a deranged fan outside his apartment in New York
14 Dec	Ten minutes of silence is observed at 7.00 pm GMT around the world in memory of John

1981

12 Jan	US release of John's single, 'Woman'/'Beautiful Boys' (16 January in the UK)
23 Feb	The LP *The McCartney Interview* is released as a limited edition in the UK and deleted the same day

26 Feb	George is ordered to pay $587,000 in damages for his unconscious plagiarizing of 'He's So Fine'. The money goes to Bright Tunes, owned by Allen Klein
13 Mar	US release of John's single, 'Watching the Wheels'/'Yes, I'm Your Angel' (27 March in the UK)
8 Apr	Paul and Linda attend the UK charity première of *Rockshow* in London
10 Apr	The world première of *Caveman* is held in New York; the film is not a success
27 Apr	Ringo marries Barbara Bach in London
27 Apr	Wings officially split
11 May	George's tribute to John, 'All Those Years Ago', featuring backing by Paul and Ringo, is released as a single in the US. The B side is 'Writing's on the Wall' (15 May in the UK)
27 May	George releases his LP *Somewhere in England* in the US (5 June in the UK)
31 Jul	UK release of George's single 'Teardrops'/'Save the World'. In the US 'All Those Years Ago' is re-issued, with 'Teardrops' now on the B side, on 4 November
28 Sept	A book that includes Paul's music, lyrics and drawings, *Paul McCartney: Composer/Artist* is published in the UK
27 Oct	Ringo releases his single, 'Wrack My Brain'/'Drumming is my Madness' in the US (13 November in the UK)
27 Oct	US release of Ringo's LP *Stop and Smell the Roses* (20 November in the UK)

1982

11 Jan	Paul's MPL Company starts shooting *The Cooler*, to promote three tracks from Ringo's LP *Stop and Smell the Roses*. Paul, Linda, Ringo and Barbara all appear
30 Jan	Paul appears on *Desert Island Discs*, for BBC Radio Four
24 Feb	Yoko and Sean attend the Grammy presentations in the US to collect the Best Album award for *Double Fantasy*
7 Mar	The BBC's Radio One network celebrates the 20th anniversary of The Beatles' first broadcast with a two-hour show called *Beatles at the Beeb*. It is broadcast in the US on 31 May 1982
22 Mar	A single, 'The Beatles Movie Medley'/'I'm Happy Just to Dance With You' is released in the US (24 May in the UK)
26 Mar	UK release of the single 'Ebony and Ivory' by Paul with Stevie Wonder, with 'Rainclouds' by Paul only on the B side (2 April in the US)
26 Apr	Paul releases his LP *Tug of War* in the US and UK
21 Jun	Paul releases his single 'Take It Away'/'I'll Give You a Ring' in the UK (3 July in the US)
20 Sept	The UK release of Paul's single 'Tug of War'/'Get It' (26 September in the US)
18 Oct	UK release of a compilation album, *The Beatles: 20 Greatest Hits*
25 Oct	US and UK release of 'The Girl is Mine', with Paul and Michael Jackson and 'Can't Get Outta the Rain' by Michael only on the B side
29 Oct	George releases his single 'Wake Up My Love'/'Greece' in the UK

1 Nov	UK release of *The John Lennon Collection*, a compilation LP (8 November in the US)
15 Nov	In the UK, EMI issue John's 'Love' as a single for the first time, with 'Give Me Some Truth' on the B side
27 Oct	US release of George's LP *Gone Troppo* (8 November in the UK)
8 Nov	Paul's film, *Give My Regards to Broad Street*, starts filming at Elstree with Paul, Linda and Ringo starring

1983

4 Jun	A 26-part series, Ringo's *Yellow Submarine: A Voyage Through Beatles Magic*, begins on US radio, with Ringo telling the story of the group
16 Jun	Ringo's LP *Old Wave* is released in West Germany. It is also issued in Canada and Brazil but no US or UK record company will take it
18 Jul	In Studio Two at Abbey Road, EMI shows *The Beatles at Abbey Road*, with rare video footage and recording session tapes. It runs for nearly two months and fans travel from all over the world
3 Oct	UK release of 'Say Say Say' by Paul with Michael Jackson
17 Oct	Paul releases his LP *Pipes of Peace* in the UK (26 October in the US)
6-7 Oct	Ringo and Barbara appear in *Princess Daisy* on US television
5 Dec	Paul releases his single 'Pipes of Peace' in the UK
5 Dec	US release of *Heart Play - Unfinished Dialogue*, an LP with bits of John and Yoko's 1980 interview for *Playboy* magazine (16 December in the UK)

1984

5 Jan	US release of John's single 'Nobody Told Me'/'O'Sanity' (9 January in the UK)
16 Jan	John and Linda are arrested in Barbados for possession of cannabis
17 Jan	Linda is arrested again at Heathrow when small amount of cannabis is found in her luggage when she and Paul return to London
19 Jan	US release of John and Yoko's LP *Milk and Honey* (23 January in the UK)
9 Mar	UK release of John's single 'Borrowed Time'/'Your Hands' (11 May in the US)
15 Mar	US release of John's single 'I'm Stepping Out'/'Sleepless Night' (15 July in the UK)
21 Mar	A plot of land in Central Park bought by Yoko is dedicated to John and named Strawberry Fields
Apr	An unauthorized double LP, *Reflections and Poetry*, containing part of the interview John gave to RKO Radio before he died, is released in the UK, but is withdrawn after Yoko takes legal action. The full interview is released as *The Last Word* in the UK in July 1988
7 Sept	As part of the eighth Buddy Holly Week, Paul presents the prizes at a Holly drawing competition in London
24 Sept	Paul releases his single 'No More Lonely Nights' in the UK
5 Oct	US release of John's single 'Every Man Has a Woman Who Loves Him' with 'It's Alright' sung by Sean Lennon on the B side (16 November in the UK)

9 Oct   A series of *Thomas the Tank Engine and Friends*, read by Ringo, is first transmitted on ITV

14 Oct   LWT's *The South Bank Show* is dedicated to *Give My Regards to Broad Street*

22 Oct   UK and US release of the soundtrack LP *Give My Regards to Broad Street*

25 Oct   The world première of *Give My Regards to Broad Street* is held in New York and Paul and Linda attend

12 Nov   Paul releases his single 'We All Stand Together'/'We All Stand Together (humming version)' in the UK only

28 Nov   In the afternoon, Paul attends a ceremony to receive the Freedom of the City of Liverpool. In the evening, the UK première of *Give My Regards to Broad Street* is held in Liverpool with *Rupert and the Frog Song* as supporting picture

29 Nov   The London première of *Give My Regards to Broad Street* is held at the Odeon, Leicester Square, attended by Paul, Linda, Ringo, Barbara and Olivia Harrison.

14 Dec   George makes an unannounced appearance with Deep Purple at their concert in Sydney

1985

18 Jan   The world première of *Water*, made by HandMade Films, is held in London. George and Ringo both have cameo roles

26 Jan   George plays guitar for a musical version of *The Hunting of the Snark*, by Lewis Carroll

11 Mar   Ringo appears in *Willie and the Poor Boys* in a cameo role

13 Jul   Paul appears in the Live Aid concert for famine relief in Ethiopia

10 Aug   Michael Jackson acquires the rights to all the Lennon-McCartney songs when he buys Northern Songs for $47.5 million

7 Sept   Ringo becomes the first Beatle grandfather, when his eldest son Zak and wife Sarah have their first child, a girl named Tatia Jane.

12 Oct   Ringo and Barbara attend the Chelsea Arts Club Ball in London

18 Nov   Paul releases his single 'Spies Like Us' in the UK

18 Nov   First UK release of John's 1971 song 'Jealous Guy'/'Going Down On Love' as a single. It is released in the US with 'Give Peace a Chance' as the B side on 19 September 1988

9 Dec   Ringo appears as the Mock Turtle in *Alice in Wonderland* on US television

1986

1 Jan   A TV special, *Blue Suede Shoes: Carl Perkins and Friends*, is shown on UK's Channel 4 for the first time. Both George and Ringo perform in tribute

24 Jan   US release of the LP *John Lennon: Live in New York City* (24 February in the UK)

26 Jan   George attends the London *Standard* Film Awards at the Savoy hotel in London, where HandMade Films picks up several awards

27 Jan   Paul receives an Award of Merit in the American Music Awards

6 Mar   George holds a Press conference at the close of shooting of *Shanghai Surprise*, along with the film's star, Madonna

15 Mar   George appears at a benefit concert for a local children's hospital at the National Exhibition Centre in Birmingham, England

21 Mar   Yoko appears at Wembley Conference Centre as part of her Star Peace world tour, which covered 33 cities in seven weeks

14 Jul   Paul releases his single 'Press' in the UK

22 Aug   US release of Paul's LP *Press to Play* (1 September in the UK)

29 Aug   A BBC TV special, *McCartney*, features extensive new interviews with Paul

29 Aug   World première in the US of *Shanghai Surprise* by HandMade Films, for which George has done the soundtrack and appeared in a cameo role

3 Sept   Paul and Linda attend the opening of a photographic exhibition on the British countryside at London's Royal Festival Hall

24 Sept   The BBC transmits a second series of *Thomas the Tank Engine* with Ringo narrating

16 Oct   The video of *Rupert and the Frog Song* picks up the 1985 Best Selling Video award at the British Video Awards held at the Grosvenor House hotel in London.

27 Oct   Paul releases his single 'Pretty Little Head' in the UK

27 Oct   US release of the LP *Menlove Avenue*, which contains previously unreleased recordings by John (3 November in the UK)

24 Nov   Paul makes a surprise appearance at the Royal Variety Performance, which is televised on BBC 1 on 29 November

1 Dec   Paul releases his single 'Only Love Remains' in the UK

8 Dec   A book of previously unpublished writings and drawings by John is published, entitled *Skywriting By Word of Mouth*

1987

26 Feb   The first four official Beatles compact discs, *Please Please Me*, *With The Beatles*, *A Hard Day's Night* and *Beatles For Sale*, are released by EMI in the UK

1 Jun   On the 20th anniversary of the official release date of *Sgt Pepper's Lonely Hearts Club Band*, Granada Television screens a two-hour documentary called *It Was Twenty Years Ago Today*, featuring interviews with Paul and George. Paul and Linda attend a party to celebrate the event

5-6 Jun   George plays two concerts for the Prince's Trust at Wembley, with guests including Eric Clapton, Ringo and Phil Collins

12 Oct   UK release of George's single, 'Got My Mind Set on You'/'Lay His Head' (16 October in the US)

17 Oct   George joins Bob Dylan for two songs of the encore during his concert at Wembley

2 Nov   After a five-year break from recording, George releases his LP/CD *Cloud Nine* in the US and UK

2 Nov   Release of Paul's CD *All The Best*, with a selection of his finest post-Beatles hits (5 December 1987 in the US)

16 Nov   Release in the UK of Paul's single 'Once Upon a Long Ago'/'Back on My Feet'

16 Nov   A series of cassettes of *Thomas the Tank Engine* stories, with narration by Ringo, are released in the UK

1988

20 Jan   George, Ringo, Yoko and Julian and Sean Lennon attend the awards ceremony at the Waldorf Astoria in New York, when The Beatles are added to the Rock and Roll Hall of Fame

25 Jan   US and UK release of George's single, 'When We Was Fab'/'Zig Zag'

2 May   US release of George's single, 'This is Love'/'Breath Away From Heaven'

26 Jun   Paul, Linda and their daughter, Mary, attend a lunch in aid of the Nordoff-Robbins Music Therapy Centre for handicapped children

11 Jul   Release of the CD *The Last Word* in the UK only, consisting of part of the interview with John at RKO radio made hours before his death

Sept   Release of 'T-shirt', a new single by Buddy Holly's old supporting group, The Crickets, which Paul has produced

30 Sept   UK release of Paul's CD *Choba B CCCP* (Back in The USSR) a collection of Rock and Roll classics originally intended only for the Russian market (29 October in the US)

4 Oct   US release of the CD/LP *Imagine: John Lennon* (10 October in the UK)

17 Oct   US release of the Traveling Wilburys' single, 'Handle With Care'/'Margarita'

18 Oct   First release in the US of the Traveling Wilburys' CD/LP *The Traveling Wilburys Volume One* (24 October in the UK)

1989

24 Feb   Release of Ringo's CD *Starrstruck: Best of, Vol 2 (1976-1983)* in the US (1 March in the UK)

21 Mar   US release of a boxed Gift Set of Paul's earlier LPs, *McCartney*, *Ram*, *Red Rose Speedway* and *McCartney II* (2 May in the UK)

10 May   US release of Paul's single, 'My Brave Face'/'Flying to My Home'

5 Jun   Paul releases a new LP/CD, *Flowers in the Dirt* in the UK (6 June in the US)

5 Jul   US release of 'Act Naturally' with Ringo and Buck Owens. The B side is 'The Key's in the Mailbox' by Owens only

23 Jul   Ringo and his All-Starr Band play a concert in Dallas to begin their 1989 world tour

26 Jul   Paul introduces his new backing band at the first of two concerts at the London Playhouse Theatre

24 Aug   US release of George's single 'Cheer Down'/'That's What It Takes'

17 Oct   George releases his LP/CD *Best of Dark Horse* in the US, featuring selections from six of his earlier LPs (23 October in the UK)

23-29 Nov   While appearing in Los Angeles during his world tour, Paul meets up again with Michael Jackson backstage after the show

19 Dec   Paul receives an award for his contribution to pop music from the Performing Right Society

1990

2-26 Jan   As part of his continuing world tour, Paul plays six nights at the International Arena in Birmingham, UK and eleven nights at Wembley Arena in London

1 Feb	Release of Paul's *World Tour Special Edition* CD
21 Feb	Paul receives a Lifetime Achievement Grammy Award
1 May	George appears in Los Angeles with Eric Clapton during the Journeyman tour
28 Jun	Paul and his band give a concert for charity in Liverpool as part of their world tour
5 Oct	George joins the Gary Moore concert on stage to play guitar
8 Oct	Ringo releases a CD *Ringo Starr and His All-Starr Band* in the UK (12 October in the US)
29 Oct	UK release of the Traveling Wilburys' CD/LP *The Traveling Wilburys Volume 3*, actually only their second album (30 October in the US)
30 Oct	A boxed set of John's songs, *Lennon*, is released by EMI in the US and UK
5 Nov	US and UK release of Paul's double-CD/triple-LP *Tripping the Live Fantastic*, featuring music from the 1989/90 tour
19 Nov	UK and US release of Paul's CD *Tripping the Live Fantastic - Highlights*, a condensed version of the 1989/90 tour
14 Dec	The CD *Testimony* is released in the UK only, containing a longer version of the RKO interview with John

1991

30 Apr	Linda launches her range of frozen vegetarian dishes in the UK
20 May	Release in the UK of Paul's CD *Unplugged: The Official Bootleg*, a performance taped during a show in 1991 and released in a limited edition of 250,000 copies (4 June in the US)
28 Jun	The world première of Paul's *Liverpool Oratorio*, by Paul and Carl Davis, is held at the Anglican cathedral in Liverpool
22 Oct	US release of the album of *Paul McCartney's Liverpool Oratorio*
11 Nov	Both UK and US release of Paul's single 'Save The Child'
1 Dec	George starts a short tour of Japan with Eric Clapton, playing at a concert in Yokohama

1992

3 Apr	Ringo is a guest presenter at the Grammy Awards in the US
6 Apr	George plays a benefit concert for The Natural Law Party at the Royal Albert Hall in London, with Ringo making a special guest appearance
22 May	Ringo releases his CD *Time Takes Time* in the US (29 June in the UK)
2 Jun	Ringo and his All-Starr Band do a concert in Fort Lauderdale, Florida to kick off their world tour
13 Jul	UK release of George's CD *Live in Japan*, recorded during the tour of 1991 (14 July in the US)
16 Oct	George plays on stage at the Bob Dylan 30th Anniversary Concert held at Madison Square Garden in New York

1993

18 Jan	Both UK and US release of Paul's EP, *Hope of Deliverance*

5 Feb	Paul begins another world tour with a concert in Docklands, London
2 Feb	Release of Paul's LP/CD *Off the Ground* in the UK (9 February in the US)
14 Sept	Ringo releases his CD *Ringo Starr and His All-Starr Band: Live at Montreux* recorded live at the Jazz Festival in July 1992
16 Nov	US and UK release of Paul's CD *Paul is Live*, with 24 live tracks including two previously unreleased new songs. It is also issued as an LP in the UK only

1994

19 Jan	John is installed as a solo artiste in the Rock and Roll Hall of Fame in Cleveland, Ohio
30 Nov	The two-CD set, *The Beatles - Live At The BBC*, is released in the UK (6 December in the US)

1995

14 Jun	Ringo and his All-Starr Band play a concert in Morioka, Japan, to begin their 1995 world tour
19 Nov	The three-part, six-hour documentary, *The Beatles Anthology*, begins on ABC-TV in the US. It is shown in six parts in the UK in December
21 Nov	The double LP, *The Beatles Anthology 1*, is released worldwide
4 Dec	The Beatles single 'Free As A Bird' is released in the UK (12 December in the US)

1996

4 Mar	The second new Beatles single, 'Real Love', is released in the UK (12 March in the US)
18 Mar	The double LP, *The Beatles Anthology 2*, is released in the UK (19 March in the US)
28 Oct	The double LP, *The Beatles Anthology 3*, is released in the UK (29 October in the US)
30 Dec	The announcement is made that Paul is to receive a knighthood

1997

26 Feb	The Beatles receive a total of three Grammy Awards, two for 'Free As A Bird' and one for *The Beatles Anthology*
11 Mar	Paul receives his knighthood from the Queen
28 Apr	Ringo and his All-Starr Band play a concert in Seattle to begin a five-week tour
6 May	Release of Paul's single 'The World Tonight'/ 'Looking For You' in the US
27 May	US release of Paul's LP/CD *Flaming Pie*
12 Aug	US release of *Ringo Starr and His Third All-Starr Band* recorded live in 1995 in Tokyo
23 Sept	US release of Paul's classical music album, *Standing Stone*
14 Oct	World première of Paul's classical symphony, *Standing Stone*
27 Oct	Release of the LP/CD *Lennon Legend: The Very Best of John Lennon* in the UK, containing John's best solo work (23 February 1998 in the US)

1998

17 Apr	Linda dies of breast cancer
16 Jun	Release of Ringo's CD *Vertical Man* in the US

20 Oct	Ringo releases a CD *VH1 Storytellers* in the US, on which he tells the story behind each song before it is performed
2 Nov	Release in the UK of the 4-CD *The John Lennon Anthology*, containing more than 100 previously unreleased tracks (3 November in the US)
2 Nov	UK release of the CD *Wonsaponatime*, containing selected tracks from *The John Lennon Anthology* (3 November in the US)

1999

15 Mar	Paul is included in the Rock and Roll Hall of Fame as a solo artiste
1 Aug	The August issue of the UK magazine *Q* publishes a readers' poll of the 100 Greatest Stars of the 20th Century, in which John comes first, with Paul second
14 Sept	Release in the UK and US of a compilation album, *Yellow Submarine Songtrack*, of all the Beatles songs featured in the film. It is released in conjunction with a restored version of the film itself
4 Oct	Release of Paul's LP/CD *Run Devil Run* in the UK, with Paul covering rock 'n' roll classics along with a couple of new songs (5 October in the US)
16 Oct	World première of Paul's *Working Classical* in Liverpool, which is performed by the London Symphony Orchestra
19 Oct	US and UK release of the LP of *Working Classical*
19 Oct	Release of Ringo's CD *I Wanna Be Santa Claus* in the US only
14 Dec	Paul plays at the new Cavern Club in Liverpool
24 Dec	George's home in Hawaii is broken into by a woman, who is later arrested
30 Dec	George is stabbed, and his wife, Olivia, injured, in the early hours of the morning by an intruder in his home at Henley-on-Thames

Bibliography

The Beatles – Hunter Davies (London, Arrow Books, 1992)

The Beatles: 25 Years in the Life, A Chronology 1962-1987 – Mark Lewisohn (London, Sidgwick & Jackson, 1987)

The Beatles Files – Andy Davis (UK, Colour Library Direct, 1998)

The Complete Beatles Chronicle – Mark Lewisohn (London, Hamlyn, 1992)

The Complete Idiot's Guide to The Beatles – Richard Buskin (New York, Alpha Books, 1998)

The Love You Make – Peter Brown & Steven Gaines (London, Macmillan, 1983)